THE BUSINESS OF

CW00324445

GETTING NOTICED

THE MUSICIAN'S GUIDE TO
PUBLICITY &
SELF-PROMOTION

James Gibson

Omnibus Press
London/Sydney

To my family – especially Chris and Laura – and friends, who love making music.

First published 1987 by Writer's Digest Books, Cincinnati, Ohio, USA

© 1987 James Gibson
This edition © Copyright 1990 Omnibus Press
(A Division of Book Sales Limited)

Edited by Chris Barstow

Cover designed by Pearce Marchbank

Cover photo by Julian Hawkins

Text art direction by AB3

ISBN 0.7119.1719.1

Order No: OP 45160

Exclusive distributors:
Book Sales Limited,
8/9 Frith Street,
London W1V 5TZ, UK.

Music Sales Pty Limited,
120 Rothschild Avenue,
Rosebery, NSW 2018, Australia.

To the Music Trade only:
Music Sales Limited,
8/9 Frith Street,
London W1V 5TZ, UK.

Typeset by Wakeworth
Printed in England by
St. Edmundsbury Press,
Bury St. Edmunds, Suffolk.

CONTENTS

ACKNOWLEDGMENTS

Lots of people helped with this book, and I thank them all. Special thanks to Carol Cartaino for giving this book the chance to get noticed, to Julie Wesling Whaley for nurturing the idea into a manuscript, and to Beth Franks, who gave coherence to the manuscript with good humour and uncanny understanding.

INTRODUCTION

Do they know who you are?

The right people, that is. Your clients, audiences, peers – people who can hire you, buy your records or songs, and help you make a living in music. Do they know who you are? And, do they know what you can do? Have they heard you lately? In fact, have they *thought about you* lately?

Do you want to make a living – or a better living – in music? Welcome, then, to a different kind of Music College, one where the hopes and dreams of every performer are met head-on by the struggle to survive. This is the world where who you know, and who knows you, is important.

Sometimes, unfair as it seems, *who* you know is more important than *what* you know. Being a good performer isn't enough. You have to practise music, of course, but you also have to practise good public relations. You have to know how to make people notice you.

"But," you say, "how can I do that? I'm a performer, not an advertising person. I don't have the time or money to prepare a publicity campaign for myself. I don't even know what's involved. What is publicity anyway, and what does it have to do with being a musician?"

Good questions. This book offers some answers.

All performers – not just musicians, but actors, jugglers, speakers, dancers, mime artists (and politicians) – have the same concerns. We all need to get noticed. It doesn't matter whether you're a classical violinist, a country fiddler, a fusion keyboardist, the lead singer in a pop group, or the leader of a dance band. You've got to find your audiences and clients and tell them what you do.

Every film star has a press officer and every recording company has an office full of publicity people. Every successful actor or actress has public relations consultants on the pay-roll. What about you?

If you can't afford the services of professional publicists, what should you do? Save your money? Forget about public relations? No. You, yourself, can make it happen.

You'll create for yourself, your band or your organisation, a publicity programme that ranges from business cards to feature articles. And you'll plan special events to call attention to your music. You'll write, photograph and record to produce exactly the materials your campaign needs, and you'll even learn how to think like a publicist – and turn ordinary events into good publicity for yourself and your group.

Big companies – and small ones – know that publicity is crucial to their success. They spend a lot of time building their publicity programmes. You can, too.

Public sentiment is everything.
With public sentiment nothing can fail,
without it nothing can succeed.

– Abraham Lincoln

PART ONE
HOW TO CREATE PUBLICITY TOOLS

CHAPTER ONE

IF YOU DON'T TELL THEM, WHO WILL?

You're a performer – a musician, a singer, an actor, a dancer. You make your living – or plan to – with your talent. You know the profession isn't easy, but it makes you happy and it's what you want to do.

The first thing you need is an audience. You could play music in your own home, of course, or for your friends, but if you're a professional you must play for others. And, if you're professional, your audience also pays you. Whether they're called clients, patrons, fans or employers, they're necessary for your success.

Your audience can be formally dressed, seated in a concert hall, awaiting your virtuoso performance with the symphony orchestra. Or your audience can be a crowded dance-floor of couples enjoying your rock band on Saturday night. Your audience may be a huge convention-hall full of people from around the world. It may be your local pub, an association, a country club, or even a group of record-company executives.

Your audience may be a corporate officer who's booking the entertainment for a training seminar. Before you can perform your music you may have to perform as a sales-person, convincing him that he should hire your group. So the first step to a profitable musical performance may be your sales performance, and it can be as important to your career as your stage presence.

Don't be Afraid to Blow Your Own Horn For most performers, working on publicity is not a luxury. It's not optional, something you do in your spare time. Getting noticed is a survival skill; if your publicity works, you'll flourish; if it doesn't, your career may not survive.

Your mother probably told you not to brag about yourself or blow your own horn too much. But the reality of the musical marketplace is different. You have to blow your own horn, pull your own strings, sing your own praises, because *if you don't, who will?*

The world is full of hungry musicians who can play with unbelievable skill. Your area probably has its share. In fact, there may be people nearby who play, sing or perform better than you. Fortunately, the real struggle for survival in the performing world isn't a talent competition alone. Much more is involved than just music. There are audiences, agents, accountants, advertisers, authors and artists to work with – and that's just the 'a's.'

The Bible warns us not to put our light under a bushel where it can't be seen. An old saying says, "The squeaky wheel gets the grease." What does that mean? It means that first, before anything else can happen, you've got to *get noticed*.

Let's say you're the best reed player around. You can sight-read fly specks from fifty paces. You have 10 thousand pounds invested in flutes, saxophones, clarinets of every description. Your intonation is impeccable, your tone pure. You sit at home on Saturday night and wonder why no one calls.

Or maybe your rock band is really superior, with a perfect blend of standards and strong original material. You have computer-driven lights, drum machines and synthesisers. Nobody hires you, and you may have to get a day job to make the payments to the music shop.

Or perhaps you just graduated from music college as a pianist and have opened a teaching studio in your home town. You know the literature, the methods. You'll be a great teacher. But you don't have any students – or income.

Professional musicians need to be noticed by the right people – band-leaders, club owners, parents of beginning piano students. But how? Should they advertise?

Probably not. In these cases, and maybe in your own, a carefully planned publicity programme can solve lots of problems and may be more effective than advertising. Publicity, properly done, creates an image that propels your career upward. It keeps your name before the right audiences. It tells the world, "This is the best musician for you to hire."

Why get noticed? At the most basic level, if they don't know you, they can't hire you. That's simple – but it's the foundation of your career.

What is Publicity?

There are basically two ways of letting people know about you and your music: you can advertise or you can publicise yourself. Advertising and publicity are two entirely different things, and each has its place. Most musicians, especially at the local level, will do very little advertising. Most musicians, on the other hand, should constantly work at creating good publicity.

Advertising is expensive. One small ad in the newspaper might cost your band hundreds of pounds. One well-done 30-second TV commercial costs thousands to produce and run. And, for reasons we'll talk about later, such ads probably wouldn't do you much good.

Fortunately, you probably don't need such advertising. What you *do* need is lots of publicity. *Publicity* includes all the ways you can get noticed without buying expensive ad space or time. Publicity makes people talk, think, read and hear about you – and it costs little or nothing.

Almost everything you do as a professional performer can be turned to good publicity, from the design of your letterhead and business cards to the production of demo tapes, from writing brochures and bio sheets to writing feature stories for newspapers and magazines. Even your hobbies and non-musical activities can play a part.

Publicity includes good client relations – the idea that the customer is always right. It involves word-of-mouth recommendations. It's usually free, but it's effective; publicity ultimately gets you jobs.

For most performers, publicity is *better than advertising*. Everybody suspects advertising because they know it's paid for, but they'll assume that the publicity they see and hear is true.

Does publicity work? Ask Tiny Tim and Madonna – and Jeffrey Archer.

As a musician, you are like every business with a product to sell. You have to find customers (in your case, an audience), and convince them they should buy the product (in your case, music). That's all there is to it – but that's a lot. This book will help, because you'll learn how to define your audience, to decide *exactly* who needs to know about you; you'll also learn how to use publicity tools and techniques to reach that precise group. Just having the tools and knowing how to use the media, however, isn't all there is to a good publicity programme. There's lots more.

We'll talk about making video and audio demo tapes. We'll discuss publicising your concerts and appearances with T-shirts, bumper stickers, posters and banners. We'll cover sales calls – the dreaded necessity. You'll learn how to make effective presentations and phone calls and how to write all kinds of letters – introduction, soliciting, confirmation and thanks. We'll even discuss advertising – the inexpensive sort that may work for you.

Getting Noticed is divided into two parts. The first is about the publicity tools you'll need, creating them yourself or finding professional help. Essentially, your publicity tool kit will include several kinds of printed materials, a few recorded items, photos and perhaps some simple advertising ideas. You'll develop a logo to identify your group and project an *image* that will help all your publicity efforts work effectively.

Part Two concentrates on using those tools to let people know what you do. These chapters discuss working with the media, writing press releases, getting feature stories about your music in the paper, calling on clients, and devising other ways to get noticed.

Throughout this book there are activities to increase your working knowledge of publicity, and add to your stockpile of helpful material. If you spend the time to do these projects, this book will help your career. While these procedures aren't perfect or magical, they do supply information and experience. Don't just say, "Oh yes, that sounds pretty interesting." Take a pencil and paper and *do the activity*. There's a lot of difference between simply thinking about something and actually getting involved.

One tool we'll frequently use is *brainstorming*. This is a simple technique, requiring nothing more than paper, a pencil and an active imagination. The idea is to create a 'storm' in your brain that will penetrate the habits that usually limit your thoughts. Brainstorming can lead to new ideas, fresh concepts, even breakthroughs.

And, throughout, we'll concentrate on how you can do it yourself – from laying out your own brochures to writing your own press releases. Why limit your creativity to music? The publicity field isn't mysterious or particularly difficult to master. Once you understand what works, you can make it work for you.

Is Your Image Right?

Your publicity tools will reflect your personality and musical ability, even when you yourself aren't around. Carefully produced letterheads, business cards, invoices, brochures, CVs, bio sheets, song lists, demo tapes, and letters demonstrate that you're a professional who knows, and cares, about your image.

What kind of image do you have? Good? Poor? Indifferent?

"Image?" you ask. "Won't reality take care of that? Why should I worry about my 'image'?"

Everybody has an image that's known by friends and, in your case, audiences. The way you dress, talk, conduct yourself, the car you drive, your demeanour, all help determine how people see you. So will your professional activities.

What do you want people to think about you? That you're the best, most professional musician in town? That you're a hard worker, an innovator, an achiever? That you're laid back, relaxed? That you're an artist who isn't concerned with business?

Why not think about how you'd like to be perceived, and work towards that goal? You can use the methods and materials discussed in this book to consolidate an image that will advance your career.

Is that dishonest? Won't you be manipulating people? Of course not. An image without underlying reality won't last. You'll never convince band-leaders that they should hire you if you can't play or don't show up on time. You'll never achieve the image of the "best party band in town" if your music isn't appropriate.

Publicity can do a lot, and your carefully cultivated image will help, but your product – music – must be of excellent quality and what your audience wants. Otherwise, all the publicity and advertising in the world won't help. Remember Sigue Sigue Sputnik.

As you read this book and do the suggested activities, remember the image you'd like to convey. At the same time, of course, keep working on your music or performance. Image without substance is as pointless as performance without an audience. Each is necessary for success.

Publicity Practice

In this activity we'll work on your image, and we'll use brainstorming as the technique to create new ideas. Take a pencil and paper, and find a quiet place where you won't be disturbed.

At the top of your paper, write something like this: "I'd like to be seen as . . . "

Now, list the qualities and attributes you'd like to have. It doesn't matter whether you have them, or are likely to acquire them. In brainstorming you don't try to be realistic. And don't worry about being silly – nobody's going to see the list but you.

Maybe you've always wanted to play rock and roll on a stage swirling with smoke-machine fog and elaborate special effects – you want to be a rock star. Or maybe you'd really like to be friends with the wealthy party people in your town, and play sophisticated show tunes at all their soirées. These ideas, wishes, hopes and dreams should be on your list.

Does your music lend itself to sophistication, or uncontrolled frenzy? Would your audience expect you to be disciplined or unrestrained? Should you be refined or macho? Do you want to be seen as living in the future – or living in the past? Do you see yourself as New Wave, or as a figure from the forties? Is your hair pink or neatly styled? Do you jump, twist and shout when you play, or is your music quiet and understated?

Obviously, this list will be unique to *you*. The beginning piano teacher will develop an entirely different image from the cutting-edge punk musician, and the dixieland banjo player will have a different image from the Musical singer. The idea is not to create a false image, but to work with the one you already have, to refine it and become aware of it as you pursue new publicity efforts.

Think about your audiences – the ones you have and the ones you'd like to have. Consider your clients. Think about your music, your talent, your general approach to life, your business goals. Write down all the ideas that pertain to the way you'd like to be seen. This will be your *image list*. Keep it. You'll use it from time to time.

Getting Noticed – the Plan Now that you're thinking about your image, here's a plan to advance it. Your publicity tools will help you to get mentioned, talked about, written about, and generally noticed in lots of media – newspapers, radio, TV and others. "But," you say, "how can *I* get this kind of publicity? I don't know any writers or broadcasters. Why would they ever notice me and my music?"

Here's a revolutionary idea: *the media need you*. Every day, radio and TV stations have hours and hours to fill. Every day, week and month, newspapers and magazines need interesting news and features. You just have to learn how to play by their rules – to give them what they expect.

Can you do this? Of course. It's done every day. The results of other people's publicity efforts are literally all around you.

Publicity Practice

Start by enrolling in the free *media university*. Get a file folder or large envelope and a pair of scissors. Every day, go through the newspaper and cut out (and save) all the articles, reviews, notices, news stories and calendar listings of arts activities in your area. Don't limit yourself to music; include plays, college activities, church projects, artists' and crafts-people's activities, and so on. Anytime you see an article about a person or group in these categories, put it in your cuttings file.

Some of these cuttings will be nothing more than the "Local band to hold bake sale this Saturday" type of listing. Go ahead and save such pieces, because you'll want similar listings before long.

Others will be full feature articles and personality profiles on individuals and groups. Some may be reviews of performances. Keep them all in your file. Eventually, you may even need several specialised files because you'll accumulate so much material. You may have one folder for sample calendar listings, another for feature articles, and a third for performance reviews.

You'll be surprised at how many articles your local paper runs about arts and community-oriented groups. Soon, you'll be among them.

As you become more expert at planning your own publicity, you'll only cut out outstanding articles and really great new ideas – but for now save everything that relates to your field – because your beginning publicity programme will need all the input you can find.

Such a growing file will demonstrate clearly that the publicity vehicles are there. Other people are getting noticed every day, and your file shows what works in your area. Your job is to do the same for yourself or your group.

Your cuttings file will be a source of ideas and inspiration. When you worry about your publicity, look at what others have done, and ask, "If they have done it, why can't I?"

You can.

What You Need to Get Started

You're going to meet lots of people and generate lots of information as you create your publicity programme. Notes, letters, articles, contracts, business cards and brochures will accumulate on your desk, in your pockets, and in your instrument case. If you keep up with this information flow you won't get frustrated. On the other hand, if you are haphazard you'll probably neglect your publicity efforts and your career will suffer.

A special, well-organised work-space will help you be efficient as you pursue publicity and career goals. Use a desk, if one's available, or clear a shelf in a bookcase, or designate the side of a counter-top or dresser as your work area. It will help if there's a telephone handy, and you'll work better if you have all your office needs at your fingertips. Sharing your work area with room-mates, or a spouse, or even children will cause you to waste time looking for files, phone numbers, cuttings or other essentials. A clean, well-lit work-place is one advantage most office workers have over people who work from home, so you should strive to create an 'office' of your own – even if it's just a drawer in the kitchen cabinet.

To stay organised from the start you need several things from the office supply shop. They include:

1. *A good diary.* Of course you have one now, to keep up with dates you've booked, but as your publicity projects get under way, you'll have lots of advance planning to do – letters, press releases, reminders to send. So get a large diary to keep track of it all – maybe a desk size.
2. *A wall calendar.* You need a quick overview of what's happening, and when. The details go in your diary or file, of course, but a large calendar quickly shows upcoming deadlines and events.
3. *A Rotodex,* or some other kind of card file. As you meet more and more people, you'll need a quick reference system for locating names, phone numbers and addresses. Many business-people use some form of the Rotodex system because it can be instantly updated and changed, but if you like three by five-inch index cards, that's fine too. Keep them in a small file box, and you'll have an inexpensive system.
4. *A business-card file.* You might prefer to incorporate business cards into your Rotodex system, or you can use a book-style business-card holder from the office supply shop. These holders have little plastic sleeves to hold business cards and are a simple way to keep up with all the cards that are now stuffed in your wallet and tossed in the top desk drawer. You'll find that business cards are ubiquitous – everybody uses them, and they'll advance your network-building activities. They won't be helpful at all, though, if you can't find them when you need them.
5. *A filing system* of some sort. You can use anything from a cardboard box to a standard filing cabinet, but you must have a system for keeping up with contracts, correspondence and notes. There are several different systems for setting up a file. You can simply file everything alphabetically, or you can set up separate sub-categories, perhaps in different file drawers or boxes, to give

different subjects their own space. For example, you might have one file for 'Publicity Cuttings,' another for 'Booking Agents,' another for 'Past Music Clients,' and so on, and file relevant material alphabetically within its category. (You'll probably find it useful to keep strictly personal material filed separately from your business data.) A good place to start your file system is your soon-to-be-bulging clip file. Set up a separate folder for 'News Stories,' 'Feature Stories,' 'Reviews,' 'Ads,' 'Calendar,' and so on. Remember: no matter what filing system you choose, it won't help you if you don't use it.

6. *A good typewriter* (or access to one). Some things *must be typed;* in many cases handwriting is just not acceptable. If you don't type, think about learning. It's not difficult, and you'll save time and money by not needing to deal with typists and secretaries.

7. *A computer.* If you have one, you already know the advantages for writing, filing and mailing. Since prices have dropped on some excellent models, you may find that an affordable computer will become indispensable to you – but don't buy one unless your business justifies it. In the beginning, especially, a computer is more a luxury than a necessity. (When you shop for a computer, be sure to check for available music programmes. Why limit yourself to word processing when the same machine will compose and print music and interface with your synthesiser?)

8. *An answering machine or service.* As you publicise yourself and build a network of contacts, it will be increasingly important for you to be available and accessible. This does not mean, of course, that you have to carry a pager and be on call 24 hours a day, but if a newspaper reporter needs to check a story detail with you, it will help immensely if you're reachable.

You need to tell the world about your music. Audiences – paying audiences – are everywhere; it's your job to find them and let them know what you do. Start by getting the right people to notice you.

CHAPTER TWO

TARGET YOUR AUDIENCE

Advertising agencies spend fortunes doing market research to locate their intended audiences – and they choose the media that reach those targets. Thus, sugar-coated cereals and toys are advertised on Saturday morning TV, and pop record albums are promoted on rock-oriented radio stations. The product suits the audience.

You should do the same thing. In your community there are thousands of people who don't really need to know about you. But there are many – tens, hundreds, maybe even thousands – who *do* need to know what you do. These will be the targets of your publicity.

So, before you start your publicity programme let's define your target audiences. Professional PR people call them *affect communities* – meaning those groups that you want to reach, to affect, with your publicity.

Thus, if yours is a rock band you probably won't need to reach the elegant gourmet restaurateurs in your area. But if you're a classical pianist or a harpist, these would be important audiences for your publicity efforts.

Or, if your band plays nothing but authentic country music, there's probably no need to tell the local community orchestra director what you do. But if you're a bassoonist, the orchestra could provide work – and a chance to enter the classical-music network that naturally leads to such related opportunities as teaching, recording or chamber-music concerts.

Your goal is to match the audience with your music. Let's say you're in a rock band. The groups you'll want to reach will include:

Booking agents
Club owners
Associations
Fair and festival promoters
Pop radio station personalities
Young (18-27) people, primarily singles

That's a good start for a target market list. But keep brainstorming and you'll come up with more categories that match your music. Ask, "Who has parties? Who buys rock records?"

Think, for example, about where your young audience shops and lives, and add those businesses to your list. They all hold openings, special sales, and other kinds of event that could use your music. Your list continues:

Record shops
Young-fashion clothing shops, boutiques
Health clubs, spas

You'll add more as your publicity plans develop; the target market list will continue to grow as your career expands, markets change, and your community grows.

Let's take another example. Perhaps you're the beginning piano teacher mentioned in the first chapter. To establish a publicity plan you first brainstorm ideas for target audiences – all the groups that need to know about your services. You come up with:

Parents of primary school children
Other private music teachers (who could give referrals)
School music teachers
Music shops

This is a start, but it's a small group, and your goal is to be known by everyone in town who could need piano lessons. As you think further about your image, however, you realise that you not only want to teach, but also want to be known as a dedicated arts leader, someone who is active in all areas of classical music. So you add community *opinion makers* to your list – people who might not be directly interested in piano lessons, but who need to know about you nonetheless. This list includes:

Amateur orchestras
College music departments
Regional arts association members
Community associations
Arts editors and reviewers for radio, TV, newspapers
Civic clubs
Amateur theatrical groups

You realise that your name must be widely known, that your network of contacts should grow, and that even unlikely groups (like civic clubs) could be productive sources of good publicity for you. Maybe the British Legion needs a programme of patriotic music performed by your students, for instance. As you learn to think like a publicity expert, you'll add other possibilities to your list.

Is that all? No, of course not. As this music teacher's career grows, she'll think of new names to add to her publicity network – more people who should know about her abilities. Perhaps the local radio station should have her on file as a classical music expert, or a teaching expert, to answer questions about issues involving those subjects. Maybe the newspaper needs freelance classical music reviewers. The possibilities go on and on for the musician who is aware of publicity potential.

An interesting thing about publicity is that you never know what results to expect – or when to look for them. Many of your efforts will be like seed, taking time to germinate and grow, but producing excellent results weeks – or months – later. If your students play that programme of patriotic music for the British Legion, it's quite possible that one of the members will remember you when his children need piano lessons. Or perhaps the local radio station will ask you to host a weekly show about great pianists. Or maybe your local TV station will decide to do a profile on your innovative teaching techniques.

One thing is certain. If they don't know about you, they won't think of you when they need a teacher, a radio personality, or a subject for their TV show.

Publicity Practice

Knowing your audiences will help you plan your publicity, because you'll know who you're talking to, who you're trying to reach. You'll be able to focus your efforts more precisely.

Start a *target audience* list of those who need to know about your music. Include both specific potential clients and those who may never hire you but should know what you do – the opinion-makers and style-leaders in your community. Since you'll be making lots of lists, and developing other publicity material, you may find it useful to keep everything together in a notebook or a folder.

Who needs your music? Who would enjoy it? Who would pay you to perform? Make your list as broad as you can, and write down every individual, group and category you can imagine. Should the mayor know what you do? Is he or she involved in planning civic celebrations and festivals? If so, add him to the list. What about the power structure of your community – the rich and influential people who give frequent parties and are mentioned weekly in the society pages of the paper? Include them. And writers, photographers and recording studios should be part of your network, too, so add them to your list. Maybe they'll never recommend you – but perhaps they will. Keep adding names. In fact, this list will remain active as long as you're in the music business, so make it a habit to add names to your *target audience* list as your career expands. As long as you perform you'll need audiences.

Define Your Publicity Goal

Now you have an idea of the image you want to project and your target audience. It's time to define your goal, to think about what publicity can do for you.

If you don't have a goal, a precise destination, you won't make the best use of your time and energy. Without a goal, any road will do; without a destination you'll never know when you've arrived.

What's your objective as you work on your publicity programme? What, exactly, are you trying to do? How can publicity help? Consider the following possibilities:

- Publicity can *get you noticed by the right people*. Whether it's concert promoters or church organists, your audience must be aware of you before they can use your talents.
- Publicity can *raise your profile*. Shouldn't all the party-givers in your community know you're the best piano player around? If your name is well-known among this group, they'll automatically think of you when they plan a party.

  Publicity can also make you a local celebrity. Do you want to be recognised by the strangers you meet? Continuing publicity will help.
- Publicity can *prove your professional competence*. If they've heard your name from lots of sources and read about you in the paper, how can your potential clients doubt your ability to do a great job?

- Publicity *builds on itself*. Each time you're on a talk show or have an article written about you, you can use that material in your future publicity projects. Each item will validate your accomplishments that much more, and provide more articles, reviews or TV clips for use in further publicity projects.
- Publicity *increases public acceptance of causes*. If you play jazz, bluegrass or classical music, your community may need to be educated about that particular style. Publicity can help raise the jazz, bluegrass or classical consciousness of potential audiences.
- The bottom line, really, is that *good, well-planned publicity can get you more work*, and make you more money.

Are you convinced? Then do the next activity and you'll be on your way.

Publicity Practice

Write down, in one paragraph, what your publicity goal is. If you can, simplify it to one sentence. Start by writing, "I want my publicity to . . ." and finish the sentence. Be specific. Don't say, "I want my publicity to make me rich and famous." Try something more like, "I want my publicity to convince people that my band is the best, most danceable pop group in town for private parties. When people think of a good time, I want them to think of Joe's Band. I want to book an average of three jobs a week."

Or, "I want my publicity to make my name widely known among people involved in education, so I can book more school concerts for my jazz ensemble. I also want teachers and parents to know that I teach privately."

Or, "I want to be seen as the most dynamic, up-and-coming cabaret-style singer around. I want to book my cabaret show into clubs, restaurants, conventions and other outlets, and to lay the groundwork for a move to the South-East. I want to collect as many positive reviews and press clippings as I can to build an impressive media kit."

Be as specific as you can. One way to do this is to think about money, and set a precise financial goal. Perhaps you want to have thirty regular students who pay ten pounds a week. Or maybe you'd like to make two hundred pounds a show. Your financial goal could be to make £20,000 a year, or three hundred pounds a week. It will help you reach that goal if you actually write it down, think about it regularly, and assess your progress toward it. If you don't get specific, you'll have no way to judge your progress.

Refine Your Publicity Goal

As you read further in *Getting Noticed*, you'll probably revise your publicity goal. That's the way it should be, because publicity isn't a one-time thing; it's a new way of thinking that will become part of your career.

Goals are important – in fact, they're crucial. But they should be realistic, too. If you try to jump from being a learner guitar player to a rock star you'll just fool yourself, and you'll certainly get discouraged. A better approach is to set yearly goals, in achievable steps. This year, for example, work on your own playing, next year join a band, and in three years plan to have an album finished. That way you can see the path, and it's not overwhelming.

Read inspirational or 'positive thinking' books, and notice the emphasis they place on goals. If you have a clear goal that's written down, you'll know where you are in your career. If you don't, you're just floating along, and probably wasting lots of time. Decide on a path, a road to follow, and do it.

The Big Hook   "All this talk about publicising my music sounds good," you say. "I'd like to be a household name and see my name in the newspaper and on TV. But – how?"

Later chapters discuss specific techniques, but one fundamental idea is so important that we'll work with it throughout this book. It's known in the public relations world as *the hook*.

You're familiar with popular music so you know what the hook is to songwriters – it's the heart of the song, the simple phrase that sums up its interest and appeal. And if you like to fish you obviously know what a hook is. It's the device that snares your prey, even against its will.

In publicity, the hook is a combination of the songwriter's and the fisherman's tools. The *publicity hook* is the item of interest that makes your music or your personality appealing to broad audiences. The hook snares their attention, catches them off guard, and forces them to become interested enough to find out about you.

So, as you develop publicity ideas, think about your music in terms that will appeal to lots of people. Watch the media to see how other people do it. You probably won't resort to burning guitars or killing chickens on stage to generate interest, but you may have to do more than simply perform your music.

Most publicity doesn't just happen. Someone has an interesting idea – and follows through. We'll talk a lot more about creating and using publicity hooks later, but for now, start noticing the publicity around you – study the *media university*. What is it that makes a story interesting? Why did the TV station bother to do a profile on that particular person? What is the focus, the slant of the magazine piece on another musician? Study the examples in your cuttings file. Watch out for the hooks. They're always there. And you can use them, too.

CHAPTER THREE

YOUR
PUBLICITY PLAN

You're ready now to work on your own publicity programme, so clients, audiences, booking agents and other musicians will start noticing you. What should you do? Randomly contact media people, visit photographers, hire printers and artists in a frenzy of activity?

No. Before you spend any time and money you should work on developing a *consistent, coherent, individual* approach that will make your publicity material work hard for you. You want a 'look' that will make each piece relate to everything else in your programme. You need an overall plan, a concept to tie everything together.

Look at the packages in a supermarket – packages that commonly cost tens of thousands of pounds to design. All the cereal boxes, say, or soup cans, or salad dressing bottles from one company have a similar 'look' that says 'Kelloggs,' or 'Campbell's' or 'Heinz'. You don't even have to read the label; just a quick glance identifies the product through colour, typography and shape.

You want to do the same thing with your publicity material. You want your cards, tape labels, brochures, even photographs to instantly say 'Joe's Band' – or whatever your name is. And you don't want it to look like everybody else's material, either.

Where do you begin to develop such an overall concept? Start with the framework – your logo.

Developing a Logo

A logo is a symbol, a graphic sign that tells people at a glance that they are reading about *you*. A logo may be as simple as your initials set in a distinctive typeface, or it may be a complex design incorporating elements of your music, your name or personality, even a slogan.

The logo is a shorthand way of identifying yourself – just as, at a glance, you recognise ICI, CBS or NEC from their corporate symbols. Since this logo will be used on all your publicity materials, and you'll use it for years, spend enough time and money to be sure it represents you as well as possible.

Your logo need not be complicated, but it should be special to you. After all, you're better than your competition – aren't you? Your promotional material should show it. Make it classy, if that's what your music is like, or make it exuberant, or exciting, or dynamic. Just don't make it average.

If you need inspiration, your library probably has books on commercial art that will give you ideas. Design magazines frequently run articles about logo design. Look at how others sum up their activities in a logo and you'll get lots of good ideas.

Here are considerations that will help you design a logo that's right for you and your music.

1. *A good logo is simple.* IBM uses only initials in a particular typestyle and a special shade of blue to identify itself. Coca-Cola uses its stylised script-like name in a particular shade of red. The simpler your logo is, the more memorable it will be and the more it will stand apart from all others.

   Your goal is to devise an emblem, a symbol that will be recognised at a glance on your envelopes, business cards, perhaps even T-shirts and stickers for instrument cases, so resist the temptation to add extraneous details, elaborate curlicues, or complex designs. Stay away from typefaces that are hard to read, no matter how 'creative' they are. People won't take time to figure out illegible script that says 'Edinburgh Baroque String Ensemble.'

   Creating a clean, simple design isn't easy. Keep working at it, leaving out as much as possible, paring your idea down to its basic components. The simpler your design, the more versatile it will be.

2. *Does your name give you ideas?* Many logos are nothing more than a name, presented in a particular way. If you're a classical player, an elegant typestyle and your full – even formal – name may be quite appropriate. ''Mark Anthony Viner, Flautist'' may be sufficient, or ''Ann Marie Smythe, Pianist.''

   Think about the parts of your name. Would just a first, or last name do? It worked for Elvis, and it's effective for Engelbert, Dion and Pavarotti. Most Johns or Susans, however will have to look further.

   What about using just initials? That's certainly simple, and, with the right graphic touch, it might provide a memorable logo. It works for PIL and REM, not to mention the LSO.

   If you're in a band with an already established name, you still need to work on developing a logo. For a rock band's visual image, you'll probably want an energetic, hip, trendy, perhaps even iconoclastic approach. Use your image sheet, and brainstorm as a group to come up with ideas that will graphically reflect your musical personality. You'll work with the group's image rather than individual ones to devise an appropriate logo – and a group identity can be difficult to pin down. Work on this until you're satisfied that your logo design represents the spirit of your band.

3. *Music is filled with strong graphic elements,* and if you can find one that accurately reflects your own performance, make it part of your logo. Consider the possibilities of keyboards, the musical staff, notation, and the shapes of most instruments – perhaps the gentle curved lines of a guitar, double bass or violin will suggest a design for your logo. A close-up view of part of a flute, trumpet or almost any instrument reveals interesting graphic possibilities.

Marc wanted a letterhead that would be memorable to advertising and music production clients, so he worked with a design firm to create these ideas. "I told them that I wanted something that was both whimsical and classy," he says, "and they presented about 40 sketches before the 'briefcase full of notes' came along. The 'composer's bust' idea was done by a cartoonist friend of mine."

Publicity Practice

Use a pad and pencil and your imagination to brainstorm the idea of a symbol for you and your music. It doesn't matter at all whether you're adept at sketching – you're after concepts, ideas and images that might work. Don't be concerned with details – simply try for several interesting designs.

Also don't worry now about the actual steps in producing the logo. Later, when we discuss typesetting, artwork layout and paste-up, you'll learn how to do it yourself or find professional help.

Whether or not you plan to actually produce the artwork yourself, you need a clear idea of what you want. Even a commercial artist will need your input. So brainstorm the logo idea until you've exhausted your creative ability.

Work on your logo design until you're really pleased with it. Then put it aside. Come back in a week or so and take a fresh look. If you still like it, go ahead and produce it, but if the perspective of a week has made your design look flat, mediocre or tacky, go back to the drawing board. You are special and your music is unique. Your logo should show it.

Your Printed Tools

When you start designing your printed materials, you'll be amazed at the available possibilities. Hundreds – even thousands – of type styles, paper and ink colours, and graphic elements are readily available. Computer typesetting machines produce an array of different typefaces, and every town has at least one quick-copy printer who will inexpensively print everything you'll need. Also, several companies make press-down lettering or press type that's available in hundreds of different type styles and sizes. Though it can be tedious to use, such press type brings almost infinite design possibilities within everyone's reach.

Quick-copy printers are a little like glorified photocopiers. All you have to do is provide clean *camera-ready artwork*, and they'll print it in any colour, on any kind of paper, in any size you need. (*Camera-ready artwork* simply refers to the material that you want to have printed, presented to the printer exactly as you want it. Artwork in this case does not mean illustrations – it simply means whatever you want printed.)

Later we'll discuss standard sizes and formats for each of these printed pieces. First, though, here's an overview of what you'll need to be fully equipped for all your publicity projects.

Your own stationery is the first step for any professional. This doesn't mean going to the printer and selecting a standard letterhead from the sample book. Use the same creative process as with developing your logo – in fact the logo should be part of all your printed material.

You'll need letter paper (A4) and matching envelopes. You might also want smaller letter paper, and perhaps a separate format for thank-you notes. All your correspondence should say at a glance, "This is from a professional who cares about appearance and detail." To make such quality obvious, you'll want to use a paper with a high rag or cotton content – and you may even choose a coloured paper.

Business cards are small and simple, but are an important part of your publicity programme. Business-people often have elaborate filing systems for business cards, and your card should be standard size to match their systems. Everyone uses, and expects to receive, business cards, so you should develop a striking design that will work for years. Use your logo, of course, to reinforce the image you're building. My card features a simple, large keyboard design, with nothing else on it but name and phone number, and people have remembered it for years. That's the kind of recall you're after – but your card has to earn such attention.

Always have cards with you, and hand them out freely. Clip one to every letter, invoice and thank-you note you send. Leave stacks of them with anyone who volunteers to recommend you – club owners, photographers, concert halls.

When you aren't around, that little 2 by 3½-inch piece of cardboard is you. Make it count.

Design can be simple or complex – both can be effective. Sometimes just a phone number is enough, as in my keyboard card.

JIM GIBSON   874·1044

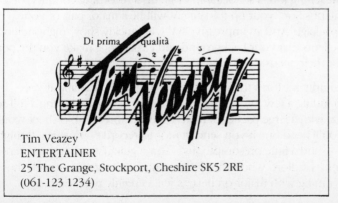

Di prima qualità

Tim Veazey
ENTERTAINER
25 The Grange, Stockport, Cheshire SK5 2RE
(061-123 1234)

Joan E. Rubin
Harpist
634-7507

Address Labels are easy to produce, and add a professional touch to your correspondence and packages. You'll need them for sending demo tapes and other publicity material, and every printer will have a variety of standard sizes. You might also have custom *audio cassette labels* printed to give your demo tapes a finished appearance – your printer will have pre-cut stock that fits any standard cassette. You can even have small stickers made, in any colour or shape, bearing your logo or a sales message, for use on envelopes, instrument cases, photos, or wherever you wish. (This doesn't include car stickers, which will be screen-printed by someone other than your quick-copy printer. They'll be discussed later.)

A few standard forms will enhance your professional image. Once you have the artwork for your letterhead, it's a simple matter to use it also on invoices and contracts.

Many clients prefer to be billed, and you'll often be paid more quickly if you send a standard invoice. Custom-designed invoices are preferable to the stock forms available at office supply stores, but your own design will cost a little more.

A printed contract form or confirmation agreement will also save lots of time. Why bother to write a letter to each client, when you can quickly fill in the blanks and have a simpler, easier-to-understand document as well? (We'll discuss contracts in Chapter Fourteen.)

Most performers will benefit by using the items listed above. We all have to write letters, send bills and use contracts, and we all need business cards and address labels. Many musicians, however, won't need all the items discussed below. If there's a chance that they'll help you get noticed, however, go ahead and prepare them. It's much easier to plan ahead and have a current CV, for example, than to stay up all night frantically trying to get one ready for an unexpected interview.

CVs are standard throughout the world of work. They simply show, in easy-to-comprehend format, who you are, where you were educated, what you've done, and what you'd like to do. They should be short and to the point, and there are several standard styles. If your only performances are with a pub rock band at the Horse and Groom on Saturday nights you probably won't need one, but if you're going after a teaching job, a scholarship or grant, a recording contract, or a classical music position, your up-to-date CV will be a major part of your information package. And an impressive CV will quickly show high-society and big-business clients that your background and experience make you the perfect entertainer for their needs.

Bio sheets simply set forth the important biographical facts about you, preferably including a few interesting anecdotes. If you're preparing a full-scale publicity blitz, with a large packet of material for the press, a bio sheet would be useful, and you'll need one if you send demos to record companies. It might be unnecessary – and a little presumptuous – for a guitarist/singer to present a bio sheet to the pub landlord who's hiring him, but a violinist who travels the country performing with major orchestras will certainly need one.

Brochures are hard-working pieces, and we'll discuss them fully in Chapter Five. Most brochures are really just one piece of paper, folded one, two or even three times to create several 'pages' or 'panels.' Your brochure will be a sales tool, telling audiences about you, giving references, and quoting past clients and reviews. It may include a picture of you or your group and will feature well-written text. There are dozens of different brochure styles and formats: you'll choose one that matches your music and personal style.

Flyers are single sheets of paper, printed on one side with an advertising message – "Joe's Band will perform at the Town and Country Club, Saturday, October 5th at 8.00 p.m. Tickets at the door." Flyers are really small posters for specific events, and can be quickly produced and distributed around neighbourhoods, on notice boards, on cars in parking lots, and on telegraph poles.

Repertoire lists sometimes come in handy. Even if they've heard you, clients invariably ask, "What kind of music do you play?" A printed sample repertoire list will answer many of their questions, and isn't hard to produce or update. For many pop and dance bands, a repertoire list is essential.

Client lists may be useful for some musicians.If you have an impressive file of satisfied clients, you may want to prepare a sheet that demonstrates your experience and association with successful organisations. If you've only worked in two country clubs in your musical life, don't prepare a client list, but if you've played for 50 major corporations and associations, why not use their prestige to improve yours? As always, however, don't lie and don't exaggerate.

Press releases are like little news stories about your activities. You'll use them to pique the interest of the local media and publicise upcoming events and musical activities. Press releases follow a standard format and aren't difficult to write; you won't even need to deal with a printer, because press releases are typed. A good press release will interest an editor, who will often assign a writer to do an article on your activities. Or, the editor may decide to print your release exactly as you've written it. Either way, it does the job and gets your story noticed. Chapter Eleven covers this important tool in detail.

Newspaper and magazine articles about you, your group or a current music-related issue can enhance your name and give you status as an 'opinion leader.' You aren't a writer? It really doesn't matter. If your band has played for 500 weddings, or if your songwriting is aided by a computer that prints out the notes you play, or if you offer free trumpet lessons to ghetto children, you will find plenty of space available for your story. You can write it yourself (as explained in Chapter Twelve) or work with a writer from a newspaper or magazine.

The press kit contains most of the material listed above, plus current photos, in a folder. Often, of course, you'll use the individual items independently, but for big projects, and to make a strong impression, you'll put everything together in the press kit. The folders can come from an office supplier, or be custom-designed and printed just for you.

A well-done press kit is a very useful piece. Even though it's just a folder, it says, "This person cares enough about her image to put together an entire packet of information about her musical activities. She's proud of her profession." A press kit is not only useful, it's impressive. We'll discuss them further in Chapter Eleven.

Newsletters are exactly what the name implies – letters bringing news – and they're a simple way to keep clients and audiences regularly informed about your activities. If you're part of a large organisation – a recording studio, college music department, or amateur orchestra, for example – a newsletter spotlights activities of the group and individual members. It gives detailed information about upcoming events and keeps your name before those who should know.

If your band, of whatever size, is active, you can use the newsletter to update club owners, agents and your local fans about developments in your group – new repertoire, equipment, dates booked, personnel changes, interesting anecdotes, and so on. In Chapter Twelve, we'll discuss getting your music publicised in newsletters published by other people and organisations.

Miscellaneous printed material includes all kinds of easily produced items. Remember, printing is available everywhere, is surprisingly inexpensive in standard formats, and produces high-quality, professional material that keeps your name before the right audiences and gets you noticed. Once you learn the simple techniques of layout and paste-up, you'll use your local printer the way you now use a copy machine. Consider the following possibilities:

● *Postcards* are useful for keeping your regular clients, subscribers, followers or fans updated on news of interest. "Susan Bennett brings her dazzling piano improvisations to the El Cordoba Café on Saturday nights. Present this card for a 10 percent discount on a meal for two."
● *Reprints of articles and reviews about you* make impressive additions to your publicity mailings. You can even make a useful promo piece from a collage of thank-you letters you've received (you do save them all, don't you?).
● *Other miscellaneous printed items* – album covers, cassette inserts, posters or banners – help reach your audience and aren't difficult to produce.

Picture Perfect

Photos are a standard part of any publicity programme. Keep your image ideas in mind when you shop for a photographer, because your photos, like everything else, must convey the feeling you want to create. The impact of your head shot can be changed dramatically by expression, pose, lighting, background, clothes and photographic technique.

You'll want a stock of up-to-date shots and group pictures, and maybe even photos of newsworthy and interesting activities of your group. You may even choose to have different photos for the different aspects of your professional life – a posed studio shot for publicity about your teaching work, and an informal, perhaps outdoor shot, for your rock band.

Photography is discussed in detail in Chapter Seven.

Demonstrate Your Ability

Your product is music – ineffable, spontaneous and probably indescribable. How can you sell a client on your band if he doesn't hear it? Do you tell him you play in tune, with a danceable beat? Do you tell him that your vocals blend so well they'll send chills up his spine? Do you tell him that your drummer never plays too loud or rushes, or that your synthesiser has a really terrific clavinet sound that's perfect for early Stevie Wonder tunes?

If you tell him any of that, he probably won't have any idea what you're talking about. Music just doesn't lend itself to translation into words, and most audiences don't share your vocabulary and concerns. Your client probably doesn't know (or care) what a clavinet is. He doesn't know that vocals should blend, and he hasn't had the piano at home tuned in 10 years.

He needs to hear your music – and he won't judge it on narrow, technical grounds, either. He'll just compare it to the records and tapes he owns – the ones produced at vast expense in the best studios in London and New York, with the world's best players. You'll have no trouble meeting that standard, will you?

Your first commitment, in planning demo tapes, must be to quality. Sure, it's easy to take a four-track machine to the job and produce a quick, inexpensive tape. But that's not good enough when you consider what you're really up against.

Remember, a tape won't capture all the excitement, the charisma, the interplay that's part of your performance, so compensate by going for top quality. In a live performance, the audience often won't notice a little intonation problem, or that the bass overpowers the keyboard. On tape, such lapses are painfully obvious.

(If you're making a pro-quality demo to sell a song or group to a record company, then quality and cost requirements will be even higher. A finished 'record quality' demo may cost several thousand pounds for one song.)

Look at Me – I'm on TV

With the prevalence of popular music on TV, the idea of music video has become an established part of the business. But before you paint your face and rush out to do bizarre things on camera, ask, "Do I *need* a video?"

The standard of 'quality first' is even more important with video than with audio demos. Why? Because today's audiences are sophisticated – they're 'video literate' from years of watching TV, and they aren't easily pleased. Again, the standard for TV quality is the 30- or 60-second commercial that is often produced without budget limitations, and often uses the best, newest, most innovative video production techniques.

Unless your band has access to quality production facilities, lots of backing money, and a TV outlet, you probably don't need a 'music video.' Think carefully about how you'd use such a one-song product, and remember that in the late eighties the average cost for a music video was around £25,000.

On the other hand, if your performance is unique and lends itself to video, you'll probably benefit from a video *demo* tape. Be sure the medium is really appropriate, that you have something visual to convey, and that you won't be just a 'singing head' (or worse yet, a 'playing head'). Television can be cruel, and even if your dance band is the best in town it may be boring to watch you standing there playing 'In the Mood.' In fact, it could be deadly.

If you're a singer with an act, a comedian, a speaker, a soloist, or you do a show, then you may need a video demo. For many entertainers, as opposed to musicians, the video demo is the centre piece of their publicity programmes.

Think carefully about whether you really need a video, and then plan it carefully and produce it well. You must be committed to quality. Chapter Eight covers videotape production.

Publicity Practice

As you work on your publicity, start a file for samples of other people's publicity pieces. Don't limit this idea file to music, but keep samples of any good brochures, letterheads, cards and stationery you see. Be alert for good group photos – from magazines or album covers. Listen for unique demo tapes, and watch TV for video techniques that you could use.

Take good ideas wherever you find them – if you like the layout and 'look' of a hotel's brochure, why not adapt the same graphic design for your use? You won't copy directly, of course, but that graphic framework, when meshed with your copy, might produce an excellent piece.

How Much Will It Cost?

If you choose to do all the publicity chores described in this book, your entire publicity campaign can cost very little – mostly materials, printing and postage expenses. You can use press type rather than a typesetter for some projects, do your own photography, and even record your own demos if you have time, equipment and knowledge. It's very possible to do an effective job of publicising your music for little more than the cost of film, recording tape and art materials.

Realistically, however, you'll probably use professionals for some publicity chores, so you'll need to devise a budget in advance. If you're a band or part of a musical group, you'll also have to decide how to pay the publicity bills. In most bands, individual members provide their own instruments and equipment, and the band may own little or nothing in common. However, since your publicity will benefit everyone, you may decide that everyone should share a fair portion of these expenses.

Once you devise a budget, perhaps each band member should contribute a percentage. If your group shares income equally, then you'll probably divide publicity expenses equally. If, on the other hand, the group's leader makes more money than the sidemen, he should certainly contribute proportionately more.

To share these expenses, and to be sure all the group members are happy, you'll need a budget. And to devise a budget, you'll have to do a little research. You'll need to decide what publicity items you'll need and whether you can produce them yourself. Then you'll need to decide what quantity you want – a hundred copies or a thousand? Finally, you'll need to carefully work out the costs of doing it yourself, and get *several quotes* from the professionals you choose to help you.

Reading *Getting Noticed* will give you plenty of information on how to produce what you'll need. But prices vary so widely that you'll have to check with local artists, photographers, printers, even PR people, to produce a budget that will reflect your needs.

Perhaps you decide that you need a letterhead, a brochure, a repertoire list, business cards, a group photo, and a well-produced audio demo tape. You'll write the brochure copy, but that's all you plan to do – the rest will be professional help. Here's how your budget might look:

Typesetting and printing for 250 letterheads and 250 envelopes £50.00
Artist's fee (including typesetting) for laying out A4 brochure and
    business-card design £125.00
Printer's cost for 500 copies of brochure, printed both sides, with two folds,
    on coated paper (one colour ink only) £70.00
Printer's charge for business cards £20.00
Photography session, including two rolls, contact prints, and three finished
    black-and-white 8 x 10's...£250.00
Mass-photo house, 500 prints with band's name added at bottom.......................£40.00
Recording studio fee for producing eighteen-minute demo master £500.00
50 duplicate cassette tapes £75.00
Total cost £1,130.00

This isn't a complete publicity kit – it's just a few of the most necessary items, and it still costs over a thousand pounds. You could, of course, lay out and design your own brochure, you might be able to shoot your own photo, and you could probably make duplicate cassettes for less than two pounds each, but you'd still have to pay the printer, photo duplication service, and recording studio. Be sure that, as you read this book, you prepare a written budget that includes everything you'll need. That way, you won't get any unpleasant financial surprises later.

Publicity Practice

Take your pad and pencil and look back at the list of publicity tools on pages 18-22. Think about your image, your career, your business. Decide which tools you'll need – letterhead stationery, invoices, demo tapes – and write each item down. If you've had experience doing layout and paste-up, you already know whether you can do it yourself. Otherwise, you may need to read Chapter Six before you decide.

Perhaps you'd like to write your own flyers and brochures, but don't think you could do a good job of design, layout and paste-up. You'll be your own writer, but will need a commercial artist's help with production. Or maybe you can write and do layout yourself, so you'll only need to find a typesetter. Do you have a terrific idea for your logo – but you can't quite get it down on paper? You need an artist. So, using the list of publicity tools as a guide, and thinking about your musical goals, list all the items you'll need. Then decide what you can realistically produce yourself. You'll probably need professional help for the rest. Chapter Nine explains how to find – and work with – artists, writers and photographers.

Looking Good

Publicity tools expand your presence and allow you to be remembered when you aren't there. Your material should be distinctive and good; it should alert people that you're a professional, that you care about your image. Before you even meet a client, prepare her by sending your press kit, demo tapes and a well-written covering letter. She'll think you're terrific, and when she meets you, or hears you, she'll already be convinced that you're a pro. That's what good publicity material can do.

CHAPTER FOUR

WRITING BASICS FOR PERFORMERS

How's your writing? "It's pretty good," you reply. "I do an occasional lead sheet, a few chord charts for the band, and I'm working on a really big project – full arrangements for a TV documentary on the history of bagpipes in colonial Massachusetts. That will really get me noticed."

Maybe it will, but another kind of writing is just as essential to your career. It's not music at all – it's writing words, and it will appeal to people who don't know a chord-change from a gear-change.

"Oh, no," you think, "not English composition again. I didn't learn about gerunds the first time around and I'm not about to do it now."

Good writing will help your publicity programme as much as anything you'll do, and you don't have to know about gerunds. It will require some care and attention, true, but it's no harder than learning the pentatonic scale.

Why Write? If you're a musician, you've probably spent hundreds of hours writing and reading music. Why should you worry about writing English, since you already speak it?

Look back at the list of publicity tools in Chapter Three. You need most of them, and someone's got to write them. It might as well be you. But whoever writes your publicity material, it must be good, because when you're not around, your writing represents you. Will your letters and brochures make a positive impression? Or will clients think you're sloppy and careless – or ignorant?

Also, your audience is barraged daily by literally *thousands* of messages – all kinds of ads, brochures, magazines, newspapers, commercials and direct-mail offers. Those bits of writing have been worked over, planned, checked and double-checked by legions of copywriters, editors, artists, photographers and PR people until they're perfect. Your printed pieces must reach that standard or they'll look amateurish.

You have to tell people what you do, who you are, why they should hire you, why your show is interesting, how you can entertain them, and why you'll do a better job than the band next door. To do this, you'll write letters, bio sheets, CVs, brochures, flyers and press releases. You might even write feature stories about your band, and, as mentioned earlier, you could produce a newsletter.

Actually, you'll find that doing your own writing isn't too difficult. Most of what you'll write will follow standard formats, so much of your task will be simply 'filling in the blanks.' We'll discuss specific aspects of writing brochures, letters and press releases in Part Two, but the ideas in this chapter apply to everything you write.

What Is Good Writing?

Good writing is any writing that does its job. Good writing communicates clearly. Good writing tells the audience exactly what you mean, leaving no room for doubt or mistakes. Good writing is direct and simple.

Good, effective writing needn't be complicated. It can be as simple as the announcement, "Joe's Band will perform Friday, June 18, at 8.00 p.m. at the Dog and Duck. Tickets at the door – £3.00." There's nothing fancy here, but the message is clear and unmistakable.

Many writers – professional and amateur alike – get very serious and stiff when they sit down to write. They use big words to sound formal, dignified, erudite, educated. They devise complex ways of saying simple things, often using several words when one would do. They end up sounding pompous and silly, and the message is often lost beneath the inflated language.

As you prepare your publicity material, remember that good writing is direct, forthright and conversational. You aren't writing a novel – or if you are, this is the wrong guidebook to use. Your intent is to communicate – not impress. Try to make your writing so transparent that it does the job without being noticed.

Good publicity writing is also informal, so avoid pomposity, complexity and inflated vocabulary. Try to write in a conversational tone, much as you speak. Use contractions. Don't seek out big words just because you're writing – you're communicating, not building your ego. Calling a lift a "vertical circulation element" doesn't impress anyone – it just sounds ridiculous.

Good writing is honest; it doesn't pretend to be something it's not. Lots of entertainers exaggerate shamelessly – but you shouldn't be among them. Most readers have a good sense of what's true and what's not, and if your publicity sounds unbelievable it won't be read. When you write, "Joe's Band performs regularly on 'The Last Resort' " be sure it's true, because someone will check. If you claim, "Susan's songs have been recorded by several chart acts," say which acts and which albums. Remember, if you exaggerate or lie outright you'll get caught. Once your credibility is questioned, it's difficult to re-establish trust.

Good writing will be understood by the target audience. You'll know a lot more about your subject – music – than your audience will, but don't flaunt it. If you need to impress people, do it musically, not verbally; don't try to overawe the reader with your education and expertise. Musical jargon and technical terms only belong in writing that's intended for other musicians.

When your band is performing a difficult work that incorporates several time signatures, is modal, changes tempo every other bar, and quotes extensively from the literature of both African folk music and Norwegian sailing tunes, you've got to be careful in writing a press release. Ask yourself, "What will my audience understand about this?" and write simply enough to be clear.

Most of all, good writing is interesting. This is where the *hook* enters the picture. Of course your music is interesting to you, or you wouldn't be doing it. The task in creating publicity items is to make it appealing to your audience. Put yourself in the readers' place. Try to imagine what will grab, and hold, their attention.

Don't tell them the details of programming your DX7 – because they don't care about algorithms. They really don't. They may be fascinated, however, by the idea that a synthesiser weighing less than three stone can sound like hundreds of different instruments, a space ship, a train and a tugboat whistle, at the push of a button. Or they may be interested in the fact that Michael Jackson's 'Victory Tour' used 14 DX7s onstage – and that you have the very same instrument in your band. Or they may be interested in the cost of state-of-the-art synthesisers, and the fact that prices are falling. You can be sure, however, that the only readers interested in details of synthesiser programming are other synthesiser owners.

Your job, as a person seeking publicity, and as a writer, is to find out what's interesting to your readers, and use it to help your writing hold the audience. If you can do that you're a good writer, whether or not you'd recognise a gerund on the street.

How to Write – The Basics

What do you do when you sit down facing that blank sheet of paper? Do you agonise over each word, strive to make it perfect the first time, worry about spelling, search desperately for the exact phrases you need? If you approach writing that way, you'll be frustrated – and you may even get a full-sized case of writer's block.

Whether you're writing a simple letter of introduction or a story about your choir's elaborate Christmas concert, here are 10 basic steps to follow that will make it easier to write anything.

1. *Know what you're trying to do.* The clearer you are about what you need to write, the easier it will be to produce it. If you're writing a business letter, look at Chapter Fourteen for more details; if you're preparing a brochure, read Chapter Five. Each item has its own customary form, and you should know what you're trying to create. Public relations writing is not free-form artistic expression.

2. *Decide what you want to say, and in what order.* First, just list everything you want to say. Write down all the subjects you need to cover. Make it simple – you're not writing a story now, just a list. When you have all the ideas on paper, arrange them in order of importance. Decide what is most crucial, most interesting, and put that first. Then move down the scale of importance on your list.

3. *Write it.* Go ahead and do your first draft. Most of the time, you'll have to revise it later; sometimes you'll even change everything. The important thing now is to get something down on paper.

   Use your list of facts from step 2, and start at the beginning. Don't worry about style, mechanics, repetition and so on. You'll clean all that up and fix the problems later. First, just *write it*.

4. *Revise it.* Wait a day, if possible, and then reread what you've written. Does it make sense? It should, of course. Is it logical – do the facts follow each other in correct sequence? If not, rework it.

   When you write anything, ask yourself, "Did I say what I meant?" "Did I say it as well as I could?" "Will anyone else find it interesting?" You may have to do several drafts to get the main points straight, and to make your ideas understandable. That's okay. Professional writers usually rewrite a piece many times. Writing is a process, not a one-time explosion of creativity; you should expect to rewrite, revise and repair until you're satisfied. If you're using a word processor, revising is much easier, but however you work, you must expect to rewrite. And rewrite. And, probably, rewrite again.

5. *Fine-tune it.* Now work on the smaller things. Try reading your effort out loud and see if you notice any problems. Look for repeated words and phrases, clichés. If you catch yourself repeating the same word – ''music,'' ''band'' or ''keyboard,'' for example – find another word, or rephrase the entire sentence. A thesaurus is handy to jog your memory, but don't use unusual, pretentious or odd words. For ''piano,'' you could substitute ''keyboard,'' ''baby grand,'' ''spinet'' or ''upright,'' depending on the context. Or you could refer to the instrument as a ''Steinway,'' or a ''Fender Rhodes.'' It would probably be inappropriate, however, to call it a 'pianoforte' – unless that's exactly what you intended.

Choosing the precise word you need is crucial to good writing – and the English language confronts you with overwhelming choices. Somewhere, you'll find just what you need, but don't go overboard – it's better to repeat ''piano'' than to make it obvious that you're searching for a synonym.

Often the ear will alert you to errors in composition and usage. Are your sentences too long? Too short? Too monotonous? If you read your work aloud, you'll know. Good word choice and varied sentence length make writing more interesting. You'll be surprised what you'll *hear* that you didn't *see* in rereading. Your musical background should help your writing's rhythm, pace and flow.

6. *Check for active verbs.* Verb phrases that use *is, are* or *were* are *inactive,* and make for lethargic writing. Relying on weak verbs is like playing every chord in the root position – it may work, but it's boring.

You'll have to read very carefully to find these tired verbs, but *is, are* and *were* are warning signs. Replace such weak phrases with stronger single verbs that add zest, spice and movement to your writing.

Look at the difference here:

''The Druids are holding auditions this Saturday morning. Anyone who is interested is invited to come along. It is necessary to bring your own music, and you are urged to be on time.''

What's wrong with that? Nothing crucial, but we can save several words, and make the announcement stronger *just by changing the verbs.* Notice the difference:

''The Druids hold auditions this Saturday morning and encourage anyone interested to come along. Bring your own music and be on time.''

The first example has 33 words; the second gets the same message across with 22. What did we lose by chopping out those extra eleven words? Nothing. What did we gain? A tighter, easier-to-read, easier-to-understand announcement.

Nothing earth-shattering, you say. True, those weak phrases and verbs didn't ruin the original announcement, but if you replace weak verbs with strong ones, your writing will be more powerful, more fun to read – and more likely to be read.

7. *Simplify, cut, reduce, pare, whittle down, eliminate.* Step seven is difficult, but very important. Go back over your piece again, and see if every word is really working for you. Almost every bit of writing can be improved by pruning. Just as too many notes obscure an elegant melody, too many words will encrust your writing – and make it deadly reading.

Here's an example from a pop band's brochure:

"You'll find that when you hire the Falcon Band your parties will be livelier, and that people will dance and have a good time. As the evening goes on, the band is capable of picking up the tempo, and moving from quiet music to today's rock and roll hits. We know hundreds of songs to suit all your moods."

Not bad, but it's not tight, energetic writing. Let's pare it down and see if we can improve that paragraph by making a few deletions and changes. When you read carefully, you'll find lots of improvements can be made.

Here's the rewritten, tighter version:

"Want a lively party? Like music that makes you dance? Then you need the Falcon Band! We'll start gently, with ballads and bossa novas, and pick up the pace when people are ready to rock and roll. From 'Stardust' to 'Shout' – we know them all."

Making changes and cutting words isn't easy, and if writing the first draft was difficult, you're going to resist cutting those hard-won words and phrases. But it has to be done. Your writing won't really suffer – it will be improved by taking out extra words, phrases, even paragraphs. Simple is often best.

8. *Use transitional words* to smooth the flow of your writing and lead the reader easily from thought to thought. You wouldn't always go from the key of F to C without the transition of a C7 chord, would you? Such words as "however," "also," "further" and "thus" do the same thing in your writing. Think of them as "dominant seventh transition aids."

Transitions improve paragraphs and sentences. Without them, your writing will seem to be a string of unrelated words and thoughts. Again, reading aloud shows where transitions are needed.

9. *Correct spelling errors.* You say, "How can I correct them if I don't recognise them as mistakes?" First, trust your instincts – if a word *looks suspicious* to you, check the spelling. Often your first impression is right – if a word looks wrong, it probably is. You can use a dictionary, of course, but you may save time by buying a little spelling dictionary that's really just a long list of correctly spelt words.

If you're using a word processor or a new electronic typewriter, you may have access to a spelling programme. Use it. Finally, have someone else read your work to check for spelling (and other) errors. You probably have a friend who excels in English who'll spot the mistakes you don't recognise.

Correct spelling is just as important as playing a melody precisely as it's written. Get it right, or you'll look careless. There's a big difference between a minim and a dotted crotchet; there's a similar difference between "capitol" and "capital."

10. *Is your writing in style?* Writing *style* refers to all the little elements that give writing its look, feel, texture. Each piece should be consistent within itself, and with the image you want to convey. If your band is on the avant-garde fringe, you'll avoid formal, studied language and try instead for a hip, contemporary tone. If your band is a middle-of-the-road group trying for country-club bookings, your style should match that audience and be responsible, factual, not too trendy. Read over what you've written, and ask, "Does this sound right for my music, my personality? Will it appeal to my audience? Will they find it appropriate? Will they read it?"

Small details are also important elements of writing style. There are several different approaches to what is 'right,' and there isn't room to cover them here. If, however, you plan to do lots of writing, you'll find there are plenty of books to help you on the minutiae of style and presentation.

For example, the correct treatment of time (one o'clock, or 1.00?), addresses (25 Church St., or twenty-five Church Street?), money (£1250.00, or twelve hundred and fifty pounds?), and numbers (twenty-seven years old, or 27 years old?) can be difficult and are usually arbitrarily decided. Since such details can vary greatly from one book to another, the best approach is to learn one system and be consistent with it.

Before we leave the discussion of style, there is one area that causes so many problems for so many writers that we'll discuss it. The problem is with apostrophes. The apostrophe has two uses. One, it indicates possession – "Anne's flute." Apostrophes are also used in contractions to replace the missing letter. Thus, "it's" means "it is." "She'll" means "she will." Avoiding contractions sounds too formal and pretentious. Don't freeze up just because you're writing.

The single most common error in writing, according to four English teachers I polled, is confusion about "its" and "it's." "It's" is a contraction, meaning "it is." "Its," *without the apostrophe in this case,* is possessive – it refers to something that belongs to "it."

When you're writing about a musical group, for example, say "Its music is so exciting that it's likely to be a sold-out concert."

The Write Stuff

When your writing is finished, revised, edited, corrected, and as good as you can make it, get someone else to read it for you. Once you've spent hours on a project, you'll be too close to it to judge accurately. You know what you wanted to say, so you can't really tell whether you've succeeded. Be sure, though, that your test reader knows what you're trying to do and understands who your audience is, for an accurate assessment.

You're going to have to write in order to get noticed. These 10 considerations will help get you started. Like music, writing gets easier the more you do it, and like music, practice makes perfect.

CHAPTER FIVE

PREPARING WRITTEN PUBLICITY PIECES

We've just discussed some important fundamentals of good writing. Now start putting them into action by preparing important publicity pieces – CVs, bio sheets and brochures. We'll discuss both content and format – because both are important. More detail about preparing written material to be printed – design, typesetting, layout and paste-up – is in the next chapter.

CVs

Not every musician will need a CV, but you may be surprised at how helpful one can be. If you're the leader of a country band looking for work at open-air events, a standard CV might not help you book the job – but it might. If you're a composer seeking funding from the regional arts association, a CV is essential. And some clients – large corporations, booking agents and record companies – need the information a CV provides.

CVs set forth, in one page if possible, your employment goal and the principal facts about you – background, education, relevant work experience, qualifications for the job you're seeking. A most important feature of the CV is its *brevity*; the reader gets a quick sense of who you are and what you've done.

To achieve this conciseness, CVs follow fairly standard forms. We'll demonstrate one here. There's no need to pay to have your CV prepared. Do it yourself, since you know the subject better than anyone else.

What should you include in a CV to give yourself the best chance?

- List relevant *higher educational achievements*. Don't tell them about grammar school unless you were the boy soprano with the symphony orchestra; emphasise recent accomplishments, including college work.
- Include *private teachers* if they are well-known specialists. "1979-81 – Studied timpani with James Blades, with special emphasis on crescendos." Or, "1985-present – Took part in workshops with Christa Ludwig."
- Include any *music awards*. If you were principal flautist of the university orchestra, say so. If you were in the National Youth Brass Band each year, mention it. If you received a scholarship to the Paris Conservatoire, list it in your CV.
- Include important *special performances* you've given. Were you invited to perform for the mayor? Did you play 'Rhapsody in Blue' with your local youth orchestra when you were 15? Did you get anywhere in a BBC "Young Musician of the Year" competition?
- List any *special repertoire* you've mastered. This only applies to very difficult show-pieces – don't list everything you know. You'll provide more detail in your repertoire list.

● Include, with dates, a list of *relevant jobs* you've held, but don't give addresses and employers' names in the CV – there isn't space. Do you play with a local semi-professional orchestra? Do you teach privately? Have you been a peripatetic music teacher in local authority schools? Did you play regularly at the local music club for years? Or was your choir featured on the local radio station?

Aim your work experience listings toward the kind of job you now want. (If you don't have any work experience, leave this category out, and concentrate on your other accomplishments.)

Publicity Practice

Before you begin work on the CV itself, make a list of the important events and dates in your educational, performing and working life. List any awards or scholarships you've received. Note special accomplishments that relate to the musical job you want.

Keep your goal in mind, whether it's teaching school music, a place in the symphony orchestra, or becoming MD of a West End show. Slant your accomplishments that way. If you change your mind next year and decide to go into banking, you'll need a different CV anyway, so aim this one at music.

You're selling yourself with a CV, so emphasise the good and leave out the bad. If you were kicked out of the Royal College for playing the trumpet out of tune, there's no need to mention that here, though you should include the dates you attended. Such careful editing of your accomplishments, however, doesn't give you licence to lie or exaggerate. Every employer will check your references and claims; carelessness with the truth will guarantee that you won't get the job.

Try to limit your CV to one page; two at the most. Edit carefully to leave out unnecessary items. Only include the most relevant, most impressive, strongest accomplishments that will help you get *this* job.

Bio

A *bio* is simply a short biography of you. Again, not every musician will need one, but if you're a guest artist, visiting teacher, workshop director, featured soloist, or a star performer, you probably will. To an extent, the bio is an expanded CV with emphasis on what's interesting and important in your life. Your bio will usually be used by writers who are looking for an angle, a slant to enliven their stories, so include anecdotes and humorous events. If you've worked at Christmas as a strolling flautist, dressed as an elf in the toy department of a department store, mention it. Or if you performed for years as a busker on the London Underground, use that information in your lead-in paragraph.

Once again, start by listing important dates and accomplishments in your life. Then write the bio in chronological order or with the most recent accomplishments first. Write in the *third person* – that is, say "John Brown studied at Hull University," not, "I studied at Hull University."

You've got to blow your own horn here, even if that's difficult. Try pretending that you're writing about someone else. You aren't after hype and you aren't writing advertising for yourself, but the bio must be interesting enough to be read. Keep it light, and fill it with the most interesting things you've done.

"John Brown spent his apprenticeship playing the sax at Leicester Square. 'The police were my most important critics,' he says ruefully. 'If they didn't like what I was playing – or where I was playing it – they'd arrest me. Believe me, I learned every officer's favourite tunes.' "

Emphasise your performance training and experience. Be factual, but not dry. Present yourself in the best possible light, but don't lie. If you have performed your 'Early Rock and Roll' show to audiences up and down the country, mention it. "Joe's 'History of Early Rock 'n Roll' show has been warmly received by audiences all over the British Isles." Be positive, but don't stretch the truth.

Include enough personal information to give writers the facts they need, but don't drag in all your family. "Joe is married and has five children, two of whom play the piano – and three table tennis." Most audiences will be interested to learn of the five children, but won't care about their names, ages and accomplishments.

If you can keep your bio to one page, that's great. If it must be longer, limit it to two pages at the most. Anything longer would seem egotistical.

Bio sheets can be typed or typeset, and should be single-spaced so all the information will fit on one page.

Repertoire Lists and Fact Sheets

Two other kinds of useful publicity material can easily be prepared by typing them on your headed paper and having them inexpensively printed or photocopied.

Repertoire lists help you answer the eternal question from prospective employers: "What kind of music do you play?" *Fact sheets* simply give the who, what, where, when and, perhaps, why of your group and your music. Both can be quickly updated, and provide a lot of information at a glance.

To devise your repertoire list, first decide what categories of music are important to your clients, and what categories you've mastered. Since you probably won't have enough space to list every song you know, pick the best, most requested, most representative and most recent tunes for your list. If you're a covers band, you'll probably want to update the list fairly frequently. On the other hand, if you're a classical harpist, your repertoire won't change very often, so your repertoire list will last a long time.

The fact sheet should simply give a quick overview of you and your music. Make it easy to read – use short paragraphs or even a list format. Don't go into detail, but stick to the most important facts you want to tell. How large is your group? How long have you been together? Where have you worked? Any special honours? Do you have a record? A show? A following? A video that's available upon request? The fact sheet is like an outline – more detail is provided by the bio, CV, brochure and repertoire list.

Brochures

One of the hardest-working tools in your publicity kit will be the brochure. It gives the facts about your music and your group. It quotes testimonial letters. It mentions your past successes, and lists prominent clients. It may include a picture of your band. It *sells you*. It does all this – but it's really only one piece of paper.

A well-done brochure tells your story briefly, and might be used for years. It isn't really difficult to produce, but it adds a finished, professional touch to your publicity material. The next chapter discusses details of typesetting and putting the pieces together; we'll discuss content and form here.

Now, what goes into your brochure? Depending on the final design you use, you'll need a cover, headline, body copy, and illustrations or photos.

You aren't writing a book. Don't tell everything you know about yourself and your music, and for goodness sake stay away from the history of your group. Clients don't want to know who had the idea to form your band, or that it fulfils a dream you've had since childhood. You must rigorously apply the *who cares?* test to everything you write.

Let's take the elements one at a time.

Cover

Your brochure will probably be one piece of paper, possibly folded twice to fit a standard business envelope. The front panel could feature a strong photo of your group, your logo, a relevant illustration, a catchy headline, or a combination of these elements. Inside, you'll tell your story in a way that makes your music seem irresistible. What you're doing, after all, is writing an ad.

Write a strong headline for the front panel of your brochure. Brainstorm ideas. Look for puns, perhaps a line from a well-known song that applies. Maybe, "We play the songs that make the whole world dance." Or, "For a good time, call – Joe's Band." Or, simply, "Joe's Band – Making Music for YOU."

Sometimes a question forces the reader to open the brochure to find the answer. Pose a question on the cover, and answer it inside the brochure. "What's the most important part of any party?" Or, "Who has helped three Lords, five mayors, a hundred major corporations, and five hundred brides and grooms dance the night away?"

Maybe you have a quote from a very satisfied client that you can use to grab the reader's attention. "Your band absolutely *made* our party. We can't thank you enough for the great music."

I saw an effective cover that was nothing more than hundreds of song titles, in small print, covering (in fact, running off the edges of) the front of a brochure, with the headline inside, "We Play Them All – and More."

Whatever you choose for the front of your brochure, remember that you have just a second or two to arouse the clients' curiosity and make them want to read further. If the cover is bland, unappealing or amateurish it will be ignored – and you won't get the job. Spend some time working on the front panel of your brochure, and get an artist's help if your own designs don't look good. (See Chapter Nine for advice on how to find and work with an artist.)

Headline

Advertising people write books about headlines, and they agonise over them daily. Look at the headlines in newspaper and magazine ads to see how they attract attention. They appeal to your *needs and desires* through questions or emotional ploys, don't they? You should do the same.

What are most clients likely to need from your music? That's what you should stress. Do they want a rip-roaring good time? Should you promise to fill the club? Will your name attract standing-room only for a concert? Will the bride and groom swoon over your wedding music? Whatever it is, emphasise it in your headline.

And work to be sure that every word is strong, and exactly right. Edit, pare it down, think about each word. If you're a wedding band, perhaps something like "Two Hundred Brides Can't Be Wrong!" would work. Or if your band specialises in fifties and sixties music, try "Joe's Band Makes You Twist and Shout!"

The headline has to grab the reader's attention – and it must do it quickly.

Copy

'Copy' refers to the text of any written piece. So now that you have their attention, what do you say about your music that will make them hire you? Follow the old advertising adage to "sell the sizzle, not the steak." Tell about the benefits, the excitement, the results of your music; don't concentrate too much on the music itself because the client won't understand.

Here's a most important idea for selling your music: *potential clients don't care about you. They care about themselves.* They really don't care that you're a terrific musician or that your band is first-rate. They especially don't care whether you need the money. What they're concerned about is how you can help them.

Tell how your music brings people together. Emphasise that your repertoire lets you play whatever the crowd wants, whether it's Richard Rodgers' 'Dancing on the Ceiling' or Lionel Richie's 'Dancing on the Ceiling.' If yours is a big band, point out that your music recreates the elegance of the thirties and forties. If you're trying for cabaret engagements, show how you work with club owners to fill the room and mention special promotions you'll do; let them know that you understand the importance of the bottom line.

Here are some ideas of what music can do for your clients. These are just samples to get you started – you should devise your own list, based on your own kind of music:

Music creates an appropriate atmosphere for any function.
Music demonstrates affluence.
Music entertains.
Music breaks the ice, encourages mixing, partying.
Music brings people together.
Music sells.
Music inspires.
Music makes people feel good.
Music attracts crowds.
Music recalls nostalgic memories.

It's important to 'think like a client' when you're writing the brochure, so you can stress the benefits that come with your music. If you really understand this fact about human nature, you'll write copy that will get results. Here's how to do it.

Publicity Practice

Get out the old brainstorming pad and pencil and start a new list. This one will cover all the ways your music benefits clients. Forget about what it does for you. What does it do, or what *could* it do, for them? Brainstorm as many ways as you can that your music will fulfil their needs. Like this:

For *pop musicians*, music creates excitement and helps clients party, mix, mingle; it also can attract crowds, fill the club, help clients make money.

Teachers can promote music as a valuable educational experience, an enjoyable and relaxing hobby, a happy group activity. It can make students 'the life of the party'; it could help them become more popular. And if they're good, they might even be able to make money at it.

For *classical musicians*, music helps the audience connect with the profound experiences of musical genius; thus it uplifts, inspires, relaxes, soothes and educates.

These are just a few of many ideas you should develop.

Next, list everything you'd like to say about your band, or your music. Remember – you want to fill the *clients'* needs. Include the outline of what you do, how large your band is, the kind of music you play (with examples), but emphasise what your music will do for the client (from your brainstorming list), testimonial quotes from past clients, a list of past clients, and selections from your repertoire list. Think about the kind of photos you'd like to include.

Now write your copy. Start with a catchy lead paragraph that asks a question or promises a benefit.

"What's the most important part of a really memorable party? Flowers? Food? Decorations? We think it's the music. Here's why."

"If you're hiring a band for your company party – watch out! You've got to please your chairman – and the warehouse staff. What band can do both?"

"Why did Ken Dodd call us 'my favourite opening act'?"

Once you have their attention, say how you can help them.

> *"Joe's Band is Bristol's most popular party band for one very good reason – we play the kind of music that everybody likes. Our five-piece group will read your crowd perfectly and pace the music to match the mood."*

> *"The Richmond Baroque Ensemble is perfect for formal occasions where elegance, history and culture are important. Our impeccable presentation of music from the sixteenth and seventeenth centuries will give your gathering the special atmosphere you want, with the added excitement of four virtuoso performers playing just for you."*

> *"Ken Dodd said, 'I always look forward to sharing the stage with Joe's Band because their enthusiasm is contagious and their music is exciting. Not only are they a great opening act, but I like their music – and they don't tell jokes.'"*

When you discuss your music, and your group, keep it short and don't say too much. Be as specific as you can. Rather than "we play all kinds of music," try "we play polkas, big band tunes, and lots of rock and roll." Actual titles often help. Remember, your clients aren't musicians, and may not really know what constitutes "early rock and roll" unless you tell them.

Be careful if you start writing too much about you, your music, your art, your need for self-expression or your creativity. Read your first draft, and count the number of times you've written "I," "we," "us" or "our." Then count the number of times you've used "you." Keep the emphasis on the client – not yourself.

Also resist the urge to write about your equipment. You're proud of your instruments and accessories, of course, but remember that it's *very, very rare* for a client to care about brands of amps, speakers, microphones, keyboards or guitars. He couldn't care less whether you use Shure, Electro-Voice or Brand X equipment. Don't tell them more than they want to know.

Your copy need not be long, but it should be lively and to the point. Use short sentences and snappy words. Don't feel that you have to fill up the entire page, either. Blank white space is an effective element of design, and uncluttered, uncrowded copy is easier to read – and more likely to be read. Testimonials work. If you have letters of thanks from past clients, quote from them or print the entire letter. Include a list of past clients, which is a kind of testimonial.

Emphasise your experience, your professionalism, your willingness to work with clients to make your music meet *their* needs.

Should you include your address and phone number in the brochure? Not if you book through agencies or other third-party employers who don't want clients to have direct access to you. Instead, simply leave a blank area on the back panel for an agent (or you) to rubber-stamp an address, or affix a sticker. If you're booking directly, just staple your business card to the brochure.

When you've finished the first draft, put it aside for several days. Come back and read it over. Get a couple of friends to read it, to see if it conveys what you intend. When you're sure it does, check it carefully for correctness.

Prices

Should you include prices in your brochure? Usually not. The brochure is a long-term publicity piece, and you don't want to be locked into today's prices if you're still using the brochure next year. Also, there are times when you need to be flexible, to have bargaining room. And, if you book through agents, they'll quote their own prices, which may be much higher than yours. Try to get your client interested in your music before you discuss the price. Use the brochure to *sell*, and save details such as cost for later discussion. When it's time to talk about money, describe your price structure in a covering letter or a separate printed price list that can easily be updated.

Photos and Illustrations

Since the photo is only a part of the brochure, it will probably be quite small. Be sure, then, that it's a close-up that clearly shows your face, and that your expression matches the tone of your brochure. If you're planning a brochure for a band, it's even more important to use a good photo, since your faces will necessarily be smaller. (Chapters Six and Seven explain what kind of photo will reproduce best.)

Photos are important, but don't use a poor one. And don't lock yourself into just one image if your style changes from booking to booking. Photos are a bit like price lists – you can easily send a supplementary one along with your brochure, and tailor the picture to the kind of client you're approaching.

Line art – illustrations that are just black and white with no intermediate grey tones – can be printed directly without the half-tone screening process and add no extra cost. So if you have a really good drawing of yourself, or perhaps a caricature, consider using it. Or perhaps an illustration is appropriate – an old-fashioned woodcut or steel engraving, for example. Don't use an inappropriate illustration just because it's available, however.

Books of copyright-free music engravings are available from Dover Publications and other publishers. You can also buy books of artwork that can simply be pasted into your layout. As long as there are no real greys – only black and white – the artwork won't have to be screened, and can be treated as line art. Old-fashioned engravings such as these could promote a historical festival or be used humorously with other publicity projects.

Format

Brochures can be simple or very elaborate. We'll only discuss the simplest form here; you can expand these ideas into a booklet if needed.

Most of the time a single sheet, perhaps folded once or twice, will provide plenty of space – and the look of a brochure – with just one trip through the printing press for each side. Look at the illustrations on page 41 of different formats for single-sheet brochures, and different ways to arrange the type. You can treat each folded section as a separate page, or panel, or you can treat the brochure as essentially two pages – front and back.

You can leave one outside-facing panel blank for address and stamp, and turn the brochure into a *self-mailer*. You may even find that a single sheet, unfolded, with a strong photograph on one side and headline and copy on the back, will suffice. This format is in effect a flyer – but with a brochure's content and impact. If well done, this simplest of all 'brochures' works well.

Whichever format you choose, try several rough drafts of different designs.

Should you run the copy vertically in columns, with a photo in the middle? Should you put the photo on the front and print the copy horizontally? Work with your typesetter, artist (if you're using one) and printer, and use your cuttings file for inspiration.

There are as many brochure designs as there are ways to fold a piece of paper. Here are some common, easy ways to turn one or two pieces of paper into effective, professional-looking brochures.

Can be vertical or horizontal

One page, two folds (A4) – offers four panels for copy, plus cover, and blank address panel.

One page, one fold (210 × 200mm) – offers two panels for copy, plus cover and address.

One page, one fold (A4) opens to full page size.

Two pages, one fold each, collated, provide eight panels, each A5 when you have lots of information.

BROCHURE FORMATS

Tell potential clients and audiences what they need to know, quickly and directly, and demonstrate that you're interested in pleasing them with your performance.

Once you start using printed material, you'll find that it's not intimidating, or especially difficult, to write and produce everything you need. If you need to update a CV to go after a particular job – no problem. If you need to prepare a current repertoire list to conform with your new band's orientation – it's easy.

And, if you need to create new printed pieces that aren't discussed here, it's no problem either, because you have the skills, knowledge and confidence to prepare good-looking publicity material that will work hard for you long after you've forgotten how hard you worked to create it.

The Press Kit While you're designing material, why not prepare a unique press kit to hold everything? Of course, you can just visit any office supply shop and buy stock folders off the shelf, but think how much better a custom folder will look.

Check with your printer for his size limitations: many quick-copy printers cannot handle a full-size folder (which is printed flat and made into a folder later). Your printer, however, can probably sub-contract the job to a 'commercial' printer with a larger press, or tell you where to get the work done. A one-colour print run of 240 folders will cost at least £150; 500 folders would probably cost 50p each, so a custom folder is a big investment.

Design the folder as you would any printed material. Use your logo or your name in an attractive type style, perhaps even in a very large size. Remember that the press kit is like an advertisement – it must be so attractive that the client will want to look inside. If you can't afford a custom-printed folder, visit a large office-supply shop and choose a plain folder in a finish and colour you like. Use your address label to personalise it, or have stickers made with your logo or name to affix to each one.

What goes into the press kit? Everything! It's a handy way to show off your brochure, photo, repertoire lists, CVs, and anything else that's appropriate. If you've collected lots of reviews and articles, include appropriate photocopies for each client.

The press kit goes to 'the press,' of course, but it's also the best way to present your material to interested clients, agents and anyone else who expresses an interest in your music. Package your material as well as you can, and it will make a positive, professional impression.

CHAPTER SIX

PRODUCING PRINTED MATERIALS

Now you know what materials you need – letterhead, brochure, bio sheet, invoices, business cards and so on – and you've considered basic writing techniques. If you're going to produce these items yourself, this chapter will show you how to transform handwritten or typed pages into handsome, hard-working publicity pieces.

First, you'll come up with a pleasing design, and have the material typeset to give it a professional look. Then you'll lay it out and paste it in position for the printer.

By Design

Books have been written on layout and design, and commercial artists work for years to develop good design skills. However, with your cuttings file for inspiration and a little practice, you can design publicity material yourself.

Look for samples of whatever format you're working on, both for inspiration and to see what the standards are. Standards, particularly for size, exist in every area, and your material should meet them unless there's a good reason to go your own way. Thus, letterheads should be A4 and business cards should be 3 ½ by 2 inches.

Use your cuttings file for ideas. If you see a good design, why not copy it? Always watch for interesting brochures, letterheads, business cards, photographs and other publicity material that looks good. Incorporate the elements you like into your own material; by the time you've changed the typeface, copy and illustrations, it'll no longer be an imitation.

Regardless of what you're designing, apply these principles:

- Simple is better than cluttered. White space is a design element too, and lots of clear space will highlight your message. Study advertisements to see how professionals do it.
- Try for balance among the different elements. If you use a block of type on the left side of a brochure, balance it with a photo, or some smaller blocks of type on the right. Let your eye be the guide; layouts can be top-heavy, side-heavy or bottom-heavy.
- Work to create a visual path through the piece. Use headlines, sub-heads, white space and graphic elements to lead the reader. Large blocks of type are deadly in promotional material, so break up your copy. Don't let your material look like a text book.
- Your logo should be an important part of most of your publicity items. A printer can make PMTs of it in different sizes for use in your layouts. (A PMT, or photomechanical transfer, is like a very good photocopy that can be printed

with no loss in quality.) You may want illustrations, and your art shop will probably have several books of 'copyright-free' illustrations that you can use.

● Photos must be *sized* and *screened* before printing. A good photo can add impact, but it must be excellent to begin with. The printing process often degrades image quality. When you're doing the actual layout, just leave the spaces blank where photos will go, and work with the printer to be sure the pictures reproduce well.

Publicity Practice

First, brainstorm for design ideas. The elements you'll use are headlines, sub-heads, body copy (that's set in paragraphs), illustrations, photographs and design elements such as boxes, dots (called 'bullets'), ruled lines and so on. These are like the pieces of a puzzle – the solution is a pleasing, coherent design.

Try several ideas for each project. Do as many rough drafts of your design as you can. Let them sit for a few days, look them over again, and continue working on the ones you still like. Try lots of combinations before you settle on a final design.

To repeat, quality is the goal. If you find that you can't get the pieces of your project to fit together in a pleasing way, find an artist to help you. You don't *have* to do everything yourself. (See Chapter Nine for details.)

Designing a brochure is like solving a puzzle: move the graphic elements around until they fit. Here, the design is on an angle to add a dynamic 'feel' to the brochure, and a photo is used. If Joe's Band were more stately or sophisticated, the brochure would probably be more formal, but here the exciting design matches Joe's music.

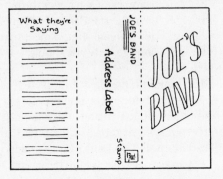

Typesetting   Your first question may be, "What's wrong with typewritten work? Why bother with typesetting?"

```
True, typewriters can produce beautiful results.
But typewritten copy doesn't look as good as type-
set work because typewriters space each letter, word
and line the same. Typeset copy doesn't--it micro-
spaces to adjust the space required to justify the
right margin--or make it even. This paragraph is
typewritten: notice the difference.
```

What needs to be typeset? Almost any printed material except letters, repertoire lists and press releases. Your typesetter will set your name and address in interesting type, and in the exact size you will need, for use on cards, letterheads, envelopes and invoices. And he will produce finished, professional-looking copy for brochures, flyers and information sheets.

Finding a good typesetter can be important to all your publicity projects, then, so approach several before deciding to work with one. Look in the Yellow Pages and ask your printer for suggestions. You could also try calling the production departments of publishing companies. Prices will vary, and so will service. Tell the typesetter about what you're doing, and let him know that you'll need advice and help. Choose someone who will work with you, even if his prices aren't the lowest, because that help will be very valuable. Often, the small, one-person businesses will be the best choices, both for service and price.

Typesetting also lets you choose from many different type styles, called *faces*, in varied sizes, densities and spacing. Most of your printing will use a few well-known typefaces because they're easy to read, but sometimes an unusual one is appropriate.

People won't work to read your material, so choose a typeface that's legible. Advertising agency research shows that type with serifs – *the little lines that decorate the tops and bottoms of letters* – is easiest to read. *Sans-serif* typefaces don't have those lines, and look cleaner and more modern, but they aren't quite as legible. Both styles, however, are popular. Good serif typefaces for general use include Times Roman, Bembo, Cheltenham, Schoolbook and Bodoni. Common sans-serif faces include Univers, Futura, Helvetica and Franklin Gothic. This book is set in Garamond.

Match the typeface you choose with your music and personal style. Different types have different connotations – symbolic and emotional values – and you should carefully assess what they are before choosing one.

A type catalogue will surprise you with the incredible variety of typefaces that's easily available. You'll find a type style that exactly matches your ideas and that will promote the image you want to project.

Helvetica Outline

Horace Light

Horace Medium

Horace Bold

Bodoni Book

Bodoni Book Italic

Bodoni Bold

Beton Extra Bold

Some faces look traditional, conservative or formal. Others seem futuristic, avant-garde, unrestrained. To show you what's available and illustrate different faces, most typesetters provide a sample book of available sizes, fonts and weights. You won't be expected to speak the language (picas, points, leading, ems), but you can use the sample book to show what you want. Your typesetter may also be able to offer valuable advice on what you should choose.

Show him a sketch of your layout so he'll know what you're trying to do. Get his ideas on type sizes for your headlines, sub-heads and body copy. If you're doing your own layout for the first time, you'll rely on your typesetter's advice and knowledge, particularly about spacing and type size. With experience, you'll develop a 'feel' for using type, but the following guidelines will help you in the meantime:

- Your finished material must be legible, and type that's too small to read will be ignored. Type is measured in *points*, a technical term; for most purposes, 10- or 12-point type will be the right size for text use. Eight points is too small and 14- to 18-point will be used for sub-heads. Larger sizes are useful for headlines, titles and even poster copy.
- Don't combine different typefaces in the same piece − the result will look confused and cluttered. In fact, try to choose a style of type that you can use on all your printed pieces; it will become your 'look', and each printed piece will reinforce your image. You can, however, use different forms of the same typeface for variety − make headlines bold, or extra bold, for example. Your typesetter will offer suggestions.
- Don't use all capital letters, except in very short headlines; words set in upper case are harder to read. And white letters on black background (called *reverse type*) are usually more difficult to read, again except for short headlines.
- Resist the urge to be graphically 'creative'. There are so many exciting, unusual and 'different' typefaces that you might decide to choose a style no one else uses. Such typefaces have specific applications in advertising and audiovisual production, for example, but would be a poor choice for your printing. Don't worry that using a common typeface will make your work look average. Being

Type that's too small can't − and won't − be read. Type that's too big won't fit the page. Your typesetter will help you select the size and style that match your needs. Ten-point type is commonly used for text, and larger sizes for sub-heads, headlines and even posters or bumper sticker design.

A − 10pt.

A − 12pt.

A − 14pt.

A − 16pt.

A − 18pt.

A − 20pt.

A − 24pt.

A − 30pt.

A − 36pt.

A − 42pt.

graphically unusual for its own sake may lead to illegible designs, and your aim is to make it easy for the reader.

Working with the Typesetter

For the best possible results, it's important to realise the typesetter is *not an editor* – his only job is to set into type the material you give him. If the copy you provide contains mis-spelt words and grammatical errors, you'll probably receive beautiful, typeset work that includes mis-spelt words and grammatical errors.

So make your copy clean, clear and legible. Don't waste your typesetter's time (and your money) by providing poor-quality originals with lots of crossed-out lines and minuscule scribbling in the margins. Write on one side of the page only, and double space between lines. Leave wide margins all around for technical typesetting notes.

Also check and double-check all copy for accuracy. All typesetters will correct their own typing errors free, but will probably charge extra for any changes, called *author's corrections*, that you make later. Read your material carefully, watching for all kinds of errors – spelling, grammar, usage. Double-check names, addresses, telephone numbers, times and dates. Some people read backwards to make errors stand out, or you could have someone else carefully check your copy. If you let it sit a day or two, it will be fresh when you come back to it, and you'll spot problems that you'd overlooked. Try very hard to catch mistakes *before they are set into type*. Remember, it's really difficult to see your own errors.

Know in advance what the typesetter's charges will be. Typesetters usually charge by the key-stroke – with computerisation, it may take several key-strokes to input a single character – and complicated formats will cost more. Prices vary enormously – one person may charge four times as much as another for the same amount of setting, depending on the level of service provided. Also bear in mind that if you want the job to be turned round overnight, it will cost you more. Always shop around, and get a firm cost estimate. You're after a top-quality, professional job, and typesetting can do more per pound for your image than anything else. Many typesetters actually do many commercial art tasks, and can help with page layout, brochure design, and even logo production. When you find a typesetter who's easy to work with, who will give you advice, whose work is nearly error-free, and whose price is reasonable, strive for a good relationship. You'll benefit for a long time.

Many printers have their own typesetters, but you may find freelancers to be less expensive. Frequently, typesetters who work for large companies will do extra work on the side, and you'll probably be able to find several freelancers nearby who have Compugraphic, or similar machines, at home.

A typesetting machine, which may cost £15,000, is not the same as a personal computer, though both have keyboards and screens. Some personal computers, however, with laser printers and the right programmes (called *desktop publishing programmes*) can produce copy that's about as good as typeset work; but always compare their quality with professional typesetting.

Alternatives to Typesetting

Typesetting is the standard way of giving your words a finished, professional look. There are, however, at least four alternatives to typesetting – transfer type, calligraphy, typing and computer printers. Each has its use.

Transfer Type. There may be times when your typesetter doesn't have exactly the type style you need. Perhaps you're designing a poster, and you need something outrageous and unusual. Or maybe you want the headline on your brochure to be in a startling typeface. In these situations, you can use *transfer type*, which comes in hundreds of different styles and sizes.

Transfer type is easy to use, but it can quickly become a tedious and time-consuming job. Only use it for doing a few words at a time – a headline, a poster or your letterhead, for example. You wouldn't want to spend the time required to use press-down letters for the actual copy of your printed pieces – it would take forever, would cost more than typesetting, and would probably look bad. Transfer type is best for applications where large letters, few words or unusual typefaces are needed.

The most common brand of transfer type is *Letraset*. Any art-supply shop will have a good selection of these typefaces and sizes, and you can easily order what they don't have. Depending on the size you buy, you'll get a large sheet that contains dozens of letters, arranged alphabetically, for around seven pounds. To use transfer type, draw a guideline with a non-reproducing blue pencil and rub the letters one at a time from the backing sheet to your layout surface.

With care and a little practice, you can produce as many headlines, posters and signs as you need. You can pick just the type style you want for your letterhead, for example, and produce it yourself. Glance through a type catalogue and you'll be excited by the possibilities for enhancing your image through creative use of type.

Graphic elements are also available in transfer form. You'll be astounded at the variety of borders, boxes, lines, decorations and even illustrations, that can easily add professional design elements to your publicity material.

Calligraphy. If your music is formal, calligraphy might be a good way to prepare invitations, letterheads, even business cards. If so, find an experienced calligrapher, and be sure that what he produces is legible, neat, clear and straight. Also, if you choose to use calligraphy or other handwritten forms, the original art should be done in black ink on white paper for best reproduction.

While calligraphy looks good for certain formal invitations, an entire handwritten brochure would probably be too much of a good thing. Remember, your goal is to be read; don't make it difficult by using an unusual handwritten style.

To find a calligrapher, you could ask at art-supply shops and art colleges. Alternatively, contact the London-based Society of Scribes and Illuminators, who will be able to put you in touch with a first-rate practitioner of the craft. Calligraphers tend to charge by the job. Charges may vary according to the complexity of your copy, so discuss exactly what you're planning with the calligrapher first.

Typewritten Material. There will be times when you'll simply use your typewriter to prepare material for publicity projects. Press releases and letters, for example, are always typed, not typeset. When typing a finished piece that will be read by your audience or clients, use a standard typeface. Even though daisy wheel and golf-ball machines offer inexpensive variety, stick to a standard typeface that looks like a typewriter – since that's what you're using. *Never* use script – it looks amateurish and tacky, and is hard to read.

Use a new black carbon ribbon – never a coloured one. And keep the machine clean. Use a toothbrush and a little solvent to keep the *o*'s, *e*'s, and other letters clear. (If you don't have cleaning solvent, you can use a little *wood* alcohol on the brush. Don't use rubbing alcohol because it contains minute amounts of oil.)

Sometimes typewritten copy looks better when it is reduced slightly before printing. If you're having copies run off at a print shop, ask the printer about a very slight reduction – it won't cost you any more, and it could improve the appearance of your material.

Desktop Printing with Personal Computers. Personal computer technology is changing so fast that you may have to read a computer magazine each month to keep up. Many personal computers with the appropriate programme and a laser printer can produce perfect typeset-quality material. These combinations require top-of-the-line machines, and are expensive, but they are creating a revolution in the communications industry.

Such 'desktop publishing' programmes not only produce typeset-quality output, but can do design chores as well. You can create forms, charts, graphs and even complete newsletters right on the computer screen, and dispense with layout and paste-up entirely.

Such programmes are much more complex, however, than the commonly available word-processing programmes. It's true that almost any printer gives access to lots of typefaces, and all word processors can justify your type (make each margin even), but word processing and desktop publishing programmes are two entirely different things.

At this writing, the Apple Macintosh is the most used desktop publishing computer, but PC compatibles will do similar tasks. However, special programmes, such as Aldus Page Maker or Ventura Publisher are required. These computers and programmes are expensive, and laser printers are also costly. Such programmes will doubtless soon be available for other popular personal computers; if you're interested in producing lots of top-quality printed materials yourself, you'll need to keep up with desktop-publishing. (Of course, if you can't afford a desktop publishing set-up, any computer with a good word-processing programme will make your *writing* chores easier.)

Finally, be careful about using dot-matrix printers for anything except rough drafts. Even with programmes that produce different typefaces, these printers still rely on tiny dots, and their quality usually isn't good enough for most publicity material. If you have one of the superior dot-matrix printers that produces 'near letter quality' type, you can use it for press releases, but be sure that the dots aren't visible. Your goal, as always, is to make it easy for the reader.

Layout and Paste-Up

Once you have your finished copy, typeset or otherwise, you're ready to lay it out and paste it up. You're going to turn those good-looking strips of copy into finished publicity pieces.

Layout is simply the task of arranging, and rearranging, all the pieces of your graphic puzzle until they look right. Paste-up is, of course, the process of pasting them down.

You'll need a few special tools.

1. *A clean, clear place to work* is essential. Layout produces lots of tiny bits of paper, some of which are important. A cluttered work-place will ensure disaster, so find a large, clean table or work surface with good lighting. Avoid the kitchen if possible – one spill can undo hours of work.

2. *Sharp scissors, and a scalpel or craft knife.* Your art supply shop will have several brands of inexpensive knives.

3. *A metal ruler and set square.* The ruler is for measuring and to use in cutting straight lines. The set square helps get everything straight, at exactly right angles.

4. *A bottle of whiting-out liquid, (e.g. 'Tipp-Ex')* can be used to clean up any mistakes. Alternatively, a razor blade or ink rubber can be used on certain grades of mounting board. Also get a blue 'non-reproducing' pencil that won't be 'seen' by the printer's camera, and several fine black pencils or pens.

5. *A light box* is handy, because layout is easier if you can see through the material you're working on. Commercial lightboxes are expensive to buy, but you can easily make one yourself. Get a two-by-four-foot scrap of frosted glass or perspex and build a box with six- or eight-inch sides to support it. Paint the inside of the box white and add a couple of fluorescent tubes.

6. *Layout or 'line' board.* You can lay your material out on ordinary card, but for extra accuracy, you can use a special board. Get the kind that has a light blue grid printed on it, and get a size that's larger than the project you're working on. If you're preparing an A4 (210 x 297 mm) letterhead, for example, be sure your layout board is at least 350 by 450 mm.

7. *Adhesive.* Finally, you need some way of sticking your pieces to the layout board. The standard adhesive for this kind of work is Cow Gum, a liquid that's applied with a brush. It's messy, and leaves residue that has to be cleaned up, but it's easy to use and is inexpensive. You can also spray mount your pieces with spray glue, which comes in a can.

   Another approach is to use hot wax to stick down the pieces. A hand-held waxer about the size of a hair-dryer melts wax and applies it to the back of your material. It can be messy, but it isn't permanent, so your layout decisions aren't final. Waxers can be quite expensive, however, so if you're working on a tight budget, you're probably better off sticking to one of the other methods.

   Don't use ordinary glue or glue sticks in paste-up, because they'll cause wrinkles and air bubbles.

Publicity Practice

Now you're ready to lay out your camera-ready art. *Always practice with photocopies.*

Never use your original, typeset copy until you're sure of what you're doing and have practised it a couple of times.

First, tape the layout board to your lightbox or table top; a small piece of tape at each corner is sufficient. Then use the blue pencil to draw an exact outline of the outside boundaries of the piece you're working on. If it's a letterhead, it's probably A4. If it's a business card, it's probably 2 by 3½ inches. Mark the centre with the blue pencil, and make guide marks outside each corner with your black pen.

Using photocopies for practice, cut apart the pieces of material you'll be working with. If you're doing a letterhead, for example, separate your name, address and phone number, and any design elements you're planning to use.

Now follow the rough draft ideas you've sketched out. Try different positions for each element of your design. When you've found a combination that's pleasing and balanced, mark the position carefully with your blue pencil.

To paste the pieces in place, use gum or wax on the back of the small pieces only – not on the layout board. Carefully put the pieces in position, making sure they're straight and square with the edge line. Use the grid on the layout board, and double-check with your set square and ruler to be sure everything is precisely in position. This is tedious, but it's very important; crooked lines will ruin your work.

To check the layout, use a photocopier. Often, you can't really judge the original because of the confused jumble of edge lines, the blue grid, and your own markings. A copy will show how the printed version will look; if you don't like what you see, now is the time to redo it.

When you've finished, and are satisfied with the practice version, repeat the process using the original typeset material.

When everything is in place, roll it flat; use a roller or a smooth glass jar or can. Start from the centre and work towards the edges, pressing firmly to squeeze out any bubbles or wrinkles.

Repeat this step with all the pieces. When you're finished, clean up the copy; you can remove little blobs of Cow Gum using a knife. The printer's camera will 'see' everything except white and light blue, so get rid of bits of glue, flecks of ink, and other imperfections. Use whiting-out liquid freely.

When you like the way your layout looks, and have checked it on a photocopier, it's ready to be printed. Protect your valuable original by taping a flap of clean white paper over it, and storing it carefully in a clearly marked envelope.

Printing It

With finished paste-up in hand, you're ready to print hundreds – or thousands – of copies so prospective employers can really start noticing you. The printer will help you with those final decisions about paper, ink and other services.

Finding a printer isn't hard – there are quick-copy shops on every high street – but finding a reliable printer who will give you advice and work with you may take a bit of shopping around.

Avoid the really big printing firms – the ones that print catalogues and four-colour brochures for large companies. You don't need their facilities, because virtually all of your printing needs can be met by a small offset printing company.

As with other services, printing costs vary a lot. When you're comparing prices, be sure that you are talking about the same paper, the same number of copies, and the same extras – such as folding and punching.

Look carefully at the samples your printer offers, to check for quality. Is the density uniform throughout? Are edges straight? Is everything precise and square? Do photographs look crisp or muddy? Does the printer seem to deliver work on time? Ask around to find out. (Many printers traditionally have difficulty with deadlines.)

Will your printer take the time to show you paper samples and discuss colours and weights with you? Will he advise you on layout?

Choosing Paper is more complicated than you'd expect. There are hundreds of different weights, textures, finishes and colours. There is newsprint, book, cover and coated paper – and all kinds of special deals. Look at lots of samples from different companies. Ask if the same paper is still likely to be available next year when you re-order.

Pick a paper that's good enough for your job, but not too good. Eighty gsm (grammes per square metre) bond is an inexpensive standard, similar to photocopy paper, without a watermark, and without much texture. It's fine for flyers, and maybe for your repertoire lists and so on, but it's not really good enough for your letterhead. Nicer papers have higher cotton, or 'rag' content, and a heavier 'weight.' Keep your budget in mind, however, and don't get the most expensive paper in the catalogue. Leave that for stockbrokers and investment bankers.

Paper 'weight' is a complex concept that's different for different types of paper. Basically, the heavier the stated weight, the nicer the 'heft' or 'feel' of the paper, but an 80 gsm bond is not the same as an 80 gsm cover or book stock. There's no need to try to understand this maze, just look at different samples to match your different projects.

Paper colour is equally complicated. You can use pastels, earth tones, 'brights,' and many different shades of white. Again, remember that your goal is communication, so don't choose a colour that will make the piece hard to read; white and the lighter shades are safest for most material, though bright colours are effective for posters and flyers.

Unless your typewriter has an automatic correction facility, try to match your letterhead colour with a standard correction fluid colour. This is more important than it may seem; if you choose an unusual paper colour, how will you correct the inevitable errors you'll make in typing? If your paper is a standard colour, mistakes aren't a problem.

Be sure exactly the same colour is available in sheets, envelopes and business card stock, so your stationery will have a uniform look. Ask the printer if this colour is established, doesn't fluctuate over time, and is always available for re-orders.

These ideas, too, will make your printing easier – and maybe save money:

● Double-check your material before leaving it at the printers. Their job is to print what you give them – *exactly as it appears*. They might notice a corner of your paste-up that comes unglued, or a line that is really crooked – but they might not; most printers are too rushed to spend time double-checking your work. Before you leave material with them, look it over one last time for cleanliness. Be sure that all the pieces are still glued firmly in place and that no smudges have appeared.

● Don't be seduced into ordering more than you need just because quantity prices are cheaper. Yes, the second thousand costs much less than the first thousand, but do you really need that many? If you move, and get a new address and phone number, what happens to all that expensive letterhead stationery? It becomes expensive scrap paper. Don't over-order.

● Printers offer other services that can make life easier. If you have several pages in a set, the printer can *collate* them for you. They can also fold, punch and even bind your work. They can *score* a line that is to be folded or cut, and can cut material to any size you need. Why spend your time folding a thousand letters in a mass mailing when, for a few pounds, the printer's folding machine will do a perfect job?

● Most jobs call for black ink, but a variety of colours is available. As with paper colour, don't get carried away by the creative possibilities – your aim is communication, and light green ink on brown paper won't help. Printers charge more for coloured ink – for the time required to re-ink the press and clean up after printing your job. Black ink will suffice for most of your printing needs, but the combination of a coloured ink with your paper stock might provide just the graphic touch that really sets your promotional material apart.

Beyond Black and White

If you're interested in going beyond simple black-and-white printing, the use of coloured ink on coloured paper stock offers unlimited possibilities. You can devise powerful combinations that look colourful and expensive for a fraction of the cost of four-colour work. Look at lots of samples as you think about paper and ink.

What if you do want to have a brochure printed, including photos, in full colour? It can be done, of course, but it is so expensive that you'll need to weigh carefully the advantages against the cost. Printing in colour requires mostly 'colour separations,' and four trips through the press. If you want to use colour, you'll almost certainly need to work with a professional designer. Though costs vary, here's a rough guide to *four-colour* – which means full colour, versus *one-colour* – which usually means black-and-white printing. If it costs about £50 to print 500 one-colour brochures on excellent coated paper, the same brochure in a four-colour version would probably cost at least £300, maybe more.

Standard sizes always cost less than unusual ones. Try to design your letterhead, card, brochure and invoice to the accepted stock sizes. You'll save lots of money that way.

Printing Photos

If you plan to use pictures in your brochure, remember that although most printers are capable of printing photos, some will do a better job than others. If you understand the process, you'll be sure that your printer will produce the high quality you need.

A printing press can only put ink on paper – black on white (or colours, of course). But black-and-white photos contain a broad range of greys, from dark to light, that offset printing can't directly reproduce. To overcome this difficulty, printers re-photograph your picture through a screen that breaks it down into thousands of tiny dots. These dots print as solid specks of black, but they can give the illusion of any shade of grey.

How? In a dark section of a picture there will be many black dots, which are perceived as a solid black area; in a light grey area of the photo, there will be far fewer dots, so the area looks grey. Look at the photographs reproduced in newspapers; it's easy to see the dots. *Screening* a photo this way turns it into a *half-tone*, and this is the method your printer will use.

Two factors, aside from picture quality (which we'll discuss in Chapter Seven), affect how well your photos reproduce when they're printed. The first is paper quality. Rough paper, such as newsprint, can't handle the minute detail required for excellent photographic reproduction; so ask your printer specifically about printing photos on the paper you've chosen. High quality coated papers are the best choice for excellent photographic reproduction.

The second factor influencing the quality of reproduced photos is the size of the screen the printer uses – finer screens produce more dots, which produce smoother tone gradations and more detail. Ask your printer what kind of screen he uses – the range is from 85 to 150 dots per inch. More dots (finer screens) produce better pictures.

Many quick-copy printers use automatic equipment that requires a relatively coarse screen, often 85 dots. They can, however, send your photos out to be made into metal plates by a sub-contractor. Though this may add to the cost, it could be worthwhile if excellent photographic reproduction is important to you.

Always ask to see samples of printed photos *using the kind of screen your printer suggests.* If they don't look crisp and clear, insist on a finer screen. Of course, the printed version of your picture can't be better than the original, so be sure to start with an excellent photo.

Printing turns your words and graphic ideas into hard-working sales tools that tell clients about you and your music. If you give the printer what he needs – clear instructions and clean camera-ready copy – he'll present you with a box of professional-looking material that will enhance your image.

Typesetting, layout and printing are important steps in creating publicity tools. Since many potential clients haven't met you or heard your music, they'll judge you by the appearance of your publicity material.

Work hard, then, to create the best material possible, so when a prospective client sees your brochure and your business card, he or she knows immediately that you're a professional who cares about detail. With such a good start, you'll be one step ahead.

CHAPTER SEVEN

FOCUS ON PHOTOGRAPHY

Prospective employers not only want to *hear* you, they want to *see* you as well. It's not that they expect you to be overwhelmingly handsome or beautiful – though that never hurts, of course – but they need to know what you look like, to be able to put a face with your name.

And, of course, photographs are such a standard, expected part of every performer's equipment that you must have a current one or they'll think you're an amateur or a beginner.

Keeping a stock of current photos takes work. You change, your group changes, and new photos must be made. You can't use that old one, no matter how good it was, if you've shaved your beard, or the blonde singer is no longer with the band.

So decide what you need and look at what you already have to see if it meets your new standards for publicity material. You know that the 'mug shot' is the staple of the entertainment industry – but do you have a good one available right now? And do you have a sparkling, up-to-date photo of your group? Further, do you have action shots of all your different musical activities? You'll need them to accompany feature stories.

You'll use this supply of photos to accompany press releases and to leave behind when you call on clients. Since your public wants to know what you look like, a good professional photograph will enhance your image. On the other hand, a shoddy, third-rate picture, or one that was obviously taken 10 years ago, will do more harm than good.

Black and White or Colour?

Most of the time you'll only need black-and-white pictures. Not only are they cheaper, they're needed more often. While national magazines and newspapers often use colour pictures, the local publications that will be your publicity outlets usually want black and white. The 8″ x 10″ black-and-white glossy is the standard of the entertainment industry, and is expected by the media, agents and clients. Black-and-white materials are less expensive for the photographer, and less expensive to reproduce. You can get either photographic or printed (lithographed) copies of your black-and-white photos made for a fraction of what colour would cost. For example, a thousand *photographic* reproductions might cost about £50 from a reproduction house, while the same number of colour prints might cost nearly £500. Even if you choose the less expensive lithography (as opposed to photographic reproduction) the cost for colour is still several times that for black and white.

It's also easier to get good quality in black and white. Creating a good colour photograph is more challenging for the photographer, and reproducing it is more difficult for printers. Stick with black and white for the easiest route to a perfect print.

What You'll Need
Here are the kinds of photographs you may need.

Head shots. Everybody in the entertainment business has one, and it's exactly what it sounds like. The head shot is a close-up of your face, and your expression is important. So are the posing, lighting and other technical factors that we'll discuss below. If you're a solo performer, a teacher, or are working for individual publicity, you'll need a good head shot. And if you're the spokesperson for your band, or make speeches, or do something newsworthy (like get a scholarship or award), you'll need a head shot to send with your press release.

Group shots. If you're part of a musical or entertainment group, you'll need a photo of the entire organisation. A good group shot is more difficult to make, because the photographer must come up with a dynamic composition that suits your music and image. And it's not easy to get four or five people to have similar expressions at the same time.

Many contemporary pop bands prefer rigorously unposed, candid photos. If this is the kind of picture your music inspires, you'll still need to be sure it's technically excellent – in focus, and with a printable range of tones. Many of the album covers that look like they were made by the singer's four-year-old child are actually professional photos – designed to look spontaneous.

Action shots. When you start working on feature stories about your music, you'll need shots of you or your group in action. Maybe it's your band playing an open-air gig. Perhaps it's you composing with your computer/synthesiser. Maybe it's your free concert at a community centre. Get pictures of anything you do that's worthy of notice.

If you're adept at photography, you can make these photos yourself, using the camera's timer or perhaps a long cable release. It's easier, though, to work with a photographically inclined friend, or even hire a photographer to make these shots – though a pro would be quite expensive. Here's where your own photographic ability can be very useful in building a photo file that covers all your musical activities. Needless to say, whenever your events are covered by a newspaper photographer, be sure to get a set of prints for yourself.

Record shots. This is the kind of photo that simply records an event. If you're named 'musician of the year,' get a photo of the award being presented. If your string quartet lands a grant from an arts foundation, get a picture of the cheque being awarded. While these photos often aren't creative, they are grist for the publicity mill, and will often be the kind of picture that newspapers print.

The Photo Session

There are, of course, several ways you can get your photo done. You can hire a professional photographer, have a friend take them, or you can shoot them yourself. There are advantages each way; the photographer has experience and can guarantee excellent results, while shooting it yourself or having a friend do it will save money. We'll discuss each approach.

If you decide to use professional help, follow the guidelines for finding a photographer in Chapter Nine. Check around, discuss prices, and look at several portfolios. When you've found a photographer you like, how can you be sure that you get the kind of photograph you need?

First, *know exactly what you want*. What's the image you want to project? Sincerity? Excitement? Youthful energy? Formality? Have a clear idea of the kind of clothes, hair-style, make-up and pose that will contribute to the right 'look' for your photo.

Here's an important concept for dealing with photographers: *you must be in control of the photo session*. The photographer, regardless of how good he is, will be inclined to make the kind of pictures he likes, that are his 'trademark.' If his portfolio contains only formal, posed portraits, don't expect him to be avant-garde with your group. Or if she specialises in high-fashion, trendy, experimental work, that's what you should expect. If you know what you want, and know that the photographer can produce that kind of shot, you're a step ahead.

One way to get the kind of photos you need is to have samples of what you want. Use your cuttings file, and look for pictures that match your ideas. *Show* them to the photographer – don't just tell him – because one picture really can be worth a thousand words.

Indoor shots, usually in the studio, are the standard, and are the easiest to control. You'll get the formal head or group shots you need inside, and the photographer can arrange backgrounds, poses and lights as she likes.

White or light backgrounds are probably best for most entertainers. Light colours reproduce better, without the danger of your hair blending in with a dark background, and they usually look more cheerful. A photo with a light background and light-coloured clothes conveys a pleasant, upbeat feeling. The opposite, with dark background and clothes, seems more serious, even sombre – though well-done, such portraits can be dramatic. Discuss these options with your photographer, and get her input on the best background for your image and her style of picture. However, avoid totally white or black backgrounds, because they reproduce poorly in newspapers and magazines.

Outdoor shots, taken on location, can be useful too. You've seen photos of rock groups standing in alleys, of string quartets posed at the concert hall, or of country bands sitting on split-rail fences. If a location is important or evocative of your kind of music, don't hesitate to use it. If you need to spend time scouting for a location, or pay a bit more to get just the shot you want, go ahead and do it – you may use the photo for a long time, and it should be as good, and as 'right' for you, as possible.

Be sure she shoots enough film to assure plenty of choices. In photography, film is the least of your expenses, so don't skimp. If you have an idea for a pose, a clothing change, a different background, or whatever, don't hesitate to try it, because if you don't get what you want from this session you'll have to come back and start over. Magazine photographers commonly shoot several rolls to get one shot, and you should keep shooting until you feel that you've got the picture you want.

When the film has been processed, you'll usually get *contact sheets* from the photographer – 8″ x 10″ sheets with an entire roll per sheet. Use a magnifying glass, or a *loupe* (a special magnifier designed for photographic viewing), to make your choices. Choose shots that are technically good (sharp, well-lit, no scratches or flaws), and well-posed (eyes open, similar expressions, good design), to have enlarged.

Posing

This is the area that separates the really good photographers from the average ones. Devising dynamic, interesting poses is not easy, but it's crucial for your group shots, and even for head shots. You don't want a static, boring line-up type picture, and you don't want your head shot to be exactly like every other portrait the photographer has made.

Of course you'll follow the photographer's directions, but you can make suggestions, too. For head shots, remember that a straight-on, frontal photo with your shoulders square to the camera is bad – it looks like the pictures on the post-office wall. You'll usually get better results if you sit at an angle to the camera, and look back at the camera. Generally, head shots are taken with the camera close to your eye level, and with you looking into the lens.

There are as many clichés in photography as in music; avoid them if possible. Coy poses with your chin resting in your palm, for example, have been done so often that they look stilted – even if they aren't. Go back to your file for inspiration.

What kind of expression is appropriate for your publicity photos? It depends on your music. You may need a cheerful, happy smile, or a warm inviting look. Or you may choose a defiant, belligerent, 'nasty' expression. You may need to use make-up, with a little lip salve on your lips – or you may not shave the day of your session so you'll look appropriately macho. Your photographer will advise about what make-up, if any, you should use. Let your picture match your music.

Group posing can be difficult. Look at the sketches of dynamic group designs on page 60. These are only suggestions, of course, and there are many other pleasing arrangements. Study the good group pictures in your cuttings file and on album covers, and notice the arrangement of bodies, heads, hands and accessories. Usually the heads, which are the centre of interest, are arranged in an S-curve, or triangle pattern, so that the viewer's eye follows a visual line from one to the next.

The worst arrangement for your band picture is the line-up shot in which you simply stand shoulder to shoulder, with everybody's heads on the same level. Of course there are exceptions and many rock groups use this arrangement because it looks unposed and very natural. If this is the look you want, use it – you can rely on clothes, expressions and posing to add interest to the static design. For most entertainers, though, a more interesting composition will result in a more interesting picture.

Look at the good group shots you see in magazines and on album covers. Usually, there is a dynamic design that leads the viewer's eye through the picture. Here are some suggested poses; you'll come up with more, depending on the size of your group. The old-style line-up shot can work, of course, but a strong composition makes it easier to get a good photo.

ANGLE

ANGLE

ANGLE

TRIANGLE

90° DROP

SINGLE LINE

"S" CURVE

"T" FORMATION

FOREGROUND

PHOTO COMPOSITION

What about photos with your instruments? Sometimes this is an effective approach, but it requires careful planning to work well because adding all those elements complicates the composition. You don't want a jumble of instruments piled together, so look for similar photos and work with your photographer to devise an interesting arrangement.

Sometimes solo performers include a bit of their instrument in a three-quarter-length pose, or even a head shot. With dramatic lighting and a good photographer, including a wind or string instrument can add interest, and class, to your photos.

If your cuttings file hasn't grown to include good examples of the photos you need, look at record albums and music magazines. *Rolling Stone*, for example, publishes a giant year-end issue that's filled with contemporary album ads and feature photos that will give you lots of ideas. Or you'll get ideas from any issue of *Melody Maker, New Musical Express, Q* or *The Face*. Photographic styles change and current magazines will keep you up to date on what's in fashion.

For classical musicians looking for graphic ideas, try *Classical Music* or *Music and Musicians*.

Remember, though, that the style, look, and 'feel' of your pictures should match your music. Just because Bruce Springsteen is photographed in a white vest doesn't mean that you should do the same. Neither does it mean you shouldn't.

Some photographers, like some musicians, work too hard at avoiding clichés. A head shot, after all, is pretty standard, and there's little room for excessive creativity. Don't resort to outlandish hair styles, unusual photographic techniques or weird backgrounds, just to be different.

If you have a good idea of the kind of picture that suits your music, and you find a photographer who can produce such shots, you'll be able to supply your clients with high-quality photos that enhance your image and help you book jobs.

Shoot It Yourself

What if you don't want to work with a professional photographer? Maybe you can't afford the rates, or perhaps photography is your hobby. You or a photographically knowledgeable friend can probably make the pictures you need. Today's cameras are so sophisticated that you can produce near-professional results without knowing an f-stop from an f sharp.

To shoot yourself – photographically, that is, you'll have to be quick, but it can be done. Most modern cameras have *self-timers* that trip the shutter 10 to 20 seconds after they're activated. You can probably run from the camera to your position in the picture in that time, but it's not easy. A similar approach is to use a long cable release that you can hold behind your back, and trip the shutter remotely.

It might be easier to work with a friend who can actually operate the camera for you. If you're the photographer in the group, you can set the camera, plan the composition, and just get your friends to take the picture and wind on the film. Shoot extra pictures in these situations, however, because they can't be carefully controlled.

Here's how to photograph yourself or your group without getting into trouble.

1. *Use a suitable camera.* To some extent, the quality of your picture depends on the size of the negative; avoid tiny formats like 110; 35mm is the smallest negative size you should use, and sophisticated 35's are very popular. You, or a friend, probably have a good camera and a couple of lenses.

   What about Polaroids? Unless you choose the black-and-white Polaroid film that also produces negatives (55PN), you'll find that these instant pictures won't provide what you need. Prints are too small, and reproduction is cumbersome.

   Generally, a good 35mm camera with a 50mm lens is good for group photos. For head shots, lenses of 100mm or so are better.

2. *Know how to operate the equipment.* This isn't a photographic textbook, but your library can provide lots of good ones. If you've decided to make your own pictures, be sure you're familiar with the camera. Know how to set it for the film you've chosen, and how to load the film accurately. Don't laugh – every photographer has horror stories of the great shots he missed because the film wasn't winding on properly in the camera.

3. *Use the right film.* You'll probably need black-and white pictures, so use black-and-white film. Choose the slowest film possible, because slower films produce finer grain and sharper prints.

4. *Shoot lots of film.* Don't limit your choices by being stingy. If you've gone to the trouble of dressing up, finding the right location, rounding up the necessary equipment, and so on, don't skimp on film. To repeat: film is the cheapest part of your photographic endeavours. Use enough to be sure you have the shot you want. You may get only one good shot per roll – or only one good shot per several rolls. That's okay – professionals don't expect each frame to be a winner, either.

5. *Be careful with exposure.* Yes, the camera has automatic exposure control, but its meter can be fooled by bright or dark backgrounds, so use a camera with manual exposure override if you can. And be careful to hold the camera still – use a tripod if at all possible. Focus carefully, and remember that longer focal lengths – telephoto lenses – require more critical focusing than do normal or wide-angle lenses. And generally, photos for professional publicity uses require more care in shooting than family snapshots.

6. *Plan your composition carefully.* Know in advance how you're going to pose the group. Scan that cuttings file, take sample pictures with you to the session, and experiment.

Try to use a simple, uncluttered background. Inside, you can use a plain wall, suspend a roll of background paper from the camera shop, or even an unwrinkled sheet or blanket. Outside, find a brick or stucco wall, or use the sky. Or you could pose your group in a car park and shoot downwards so that the asphalt provides a plain background. Using a large (low number) f-stop ensures that the background will be out of focus and less distracting.

Static pictures look dead. The exact centre of a photo is boring; slight offsets to one side are more dynamic. Don't divide the space right down the middle, for the same reason. Use the triangle or S-curve composition discussed above.

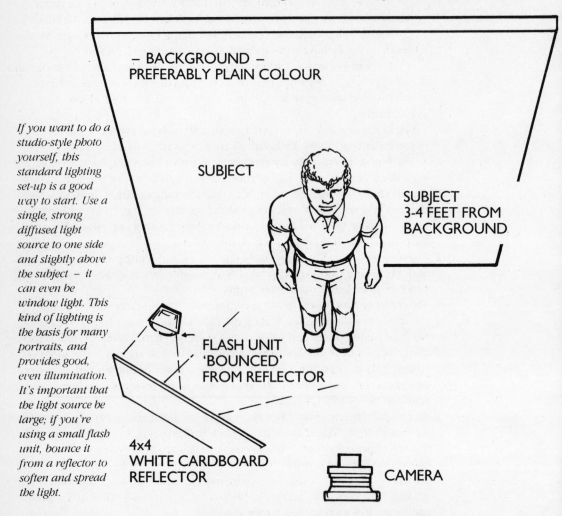

If you want to do a studio-style photo yourself, this standard lighting set-up is a good way to start. Use a single, strong diffused light source to one side and slightly above the subject – it can even be window light. This kind of lighting is the basis for many portraits, and provides good, even illumination. It's important that the light source be large; if you're using a small flash unit, bounce it from a reflector to soften and spread the light.

– BACKGROUND –
PREFERABLY PLAIN COLOUR

SUBJECT

SUBJECT
3-4 FEET FROM
BACKGROUND

FLASH UNIT
'BOUNCED'
FROM REFLECTOR

4x4
WHITE CARDBOARD
REFLECTOR

CAMERA

BASIC PORTRAIT LIGHTING SET-UP

You might try having one person seated, one kneeling, and others standing to get the variety of head heights that you need. Again, don't stand facing the camera; place bodies at angles to the lens rather than facing in frontally.

Group shots look better when people are closer together than normal. Check your sample photos – see how the shoulders usually touch, how the heads are close together?

Poses are important. Try several. Even though you're shooting lots of film, don't make exact duplicates. Vary your positions, change the hands, tilt the heads differently, change the angle of the body, and try different expressions. You'll develop a feeling for compositions that look good. Look at the illustrations on page 60 of different posing ideas – notice how the groups are arranged so the viewer's eye will travel around the picture. Strive for dynamic poses; work to avoid those tired, static clichés.

If you're using flash, don't keep it on the camera unless you're after a harsh documentary-style look. It's better to bounce it off a wall or ceiling, or from a large white reflector (a four-foot square of painted cardboard works well). Standard portrait lighting, from time immemorial, is to have the main – often the only – light positioned slightly above and to one side of the subject. It worked for Rembrandt, and it will work for you.

Don't skimp on processing. Find a local lab that does custom black-and-white work; avoid budget processing. Get contact sheets made, and look at them with a magnifying glass to make your print selection. Mass-market processing may be fine, but why take risks after you've spent all that time and effort? Custom labs will be more careful with your film, and will usually do a much better job of processing and printing.

Activity Pictures

Keep a photographic log of all your musical activities. As you become more expert at public relations, you'll devise lots of events that can be publicised, and you'll need good photos of these events. If you're trying for a feature story in the local paper, your chances will be better if you provide a few top-quality pictures.

First, learn to think like a feature writer. Whatever you do musically that could be interesting to the public should be photographed. Maybe your piano students are giving a recital, dressed up like famous composers. You should have pictures of this event – even if you have no immediate publicity plans for them. Cover yourself for future ideas.

When shooting feature photos, cover the entire story – beginning, middle and end. Perhaps your local paper will run a complete picture story on your activity; in any case, the more pictures you provide, the more choices the editor will have.

Since the most important subjects in most feature photos are people, emphasise the human element. Do close-ups of faces, hands, fingers on keys. Get close group shots. Look for dynamic interaction, interesting expressions. If you're doing a story about your collection of early electric guitars, try a picture holding that early Stratocaster – or sitting on the floor surrounded by guitars. Be creative, but not outlandish – editors won't print weird, or poor, photos.

Use your cuttings file for inspiration, and remember that a picture often brings a story to life. If you can do it yourself, fine, but hire a photographer if you need to. The pictures will pay for themselves in good publicity for you.

Whenever you get an award, give a speech, are a guest soloist, or play a recital, have photos made. Call the newspaper in advance and ask for a photographer to be sent. If they assign one, ask about buying a few prints. If no photographer has been scheduled, ask a friend to make pictures or hire a photographer yourself. It might seem pushy, but a photo of you getting the 'Songwriter of the Year Award' could run in several papers and even a few magazines. Don't miss these photo opportunities.

Such shots won't win any photographic awards, but they are important. If your band is signing a record contract, get a picture – even if it's nothing more than five people crowded around a desk looking at a contract. Watch your local papers; these are the kinds of photos that get printed by the thousands – because they show people doing important or interesting things.

If you're taking these pictures yourself, or having an amateur photographer do them, keep these ideas in mind: look behind the subject for distractions – avoid busy backgrounds when possible. When a wall is the background, stand three or four feet in front of it, not right against it, to avoid harsh shadows. Try to keep the camera on eye level with the subjects; shooting from below is an unattractive angle. Don't shoot into a mirror or window – your flash will reflect and ruin the picture. If you're using the self-timer to shoot a picture that you'll be in, carefully visualise where you'll stand and be sure that that part of the picture is in focus, and that your head won't be 'cut off' because you're so tall.

Be familiar with your camera *before* you try to take important pictures. Shoot a roll or two in different situations for practice. If you're interested in photography, take a course or get advice from a more experienced friend. Photography is a great hobby, and when you use it to get noticed in your profession, it's a tax-deductible business expense as well!

The Prints You'll Need

For years, the 8″ x 10″ glossy has been the standard, and it's still the best size for all-round use. You can send them with press releases, give them to club managers, and include them in your press kit and with material you send to prospective employers.

The best way to buy quantity prints is to use a photographic processor; check your Yellow Pages for local companies. Get your photographer to make one or two excellent prints of each pose you select, and send those pictures (not negatives) to the processor. They'll add your name at the bottom, in whatever type style you select, and make hundreds – or thousands – of 'dupe' prints for you at a fraction of what your photographer would charge. (This is not unethical – all photographers know that duplication is the best route for anyone who needs large numbers of prints – though if you only need a print or two, buy those from your photographer, of course.)

If you're doing a large mailing of press releases, 5″ x 7″ prints will be acceptable and will save money over the larger size.

If you need lots of photos, check into litho prints, which are produced on a printing press rather than in the darkroom. Good quality lithos, on coated stock, look almost as good as photos, and are considerably less expensive.

Using Photos

Once you have a stack of new head shots and a file full of feature photos of your band's activities, how do you distribute them?

First, be sure they're labelled. An editor of a large paper will receive dozens – maybe hundreds – of pictures every day. He won't spend time searching his desktop to find the photos that match your press release. All photos sent out *must be labelled.*

If your head shot has your name printed on the bottom, that's sufficient. For other pictures, type the names (from left to right) and other pertinent data across the bottom of a piece of paper that's as wide as the picture, and tape it to the back of the photo. Fold the caption over the bottom of the picture, so that it reads right when it's unfolded. Or you can type the caption and names (left to right) on a self-adhesive label, and stick it to the back of the photo.

Never write on the back of a photo and never use paper clips on a picture. Any indentations will show when the photo is reproduced, and such carelessness may result in the photo being discarded rather than used.

When you're ordering prints to be used in a newspaper or magazine, ask the photographer to make them 'flatter,' with less contrast than normal, since printing adds contrast. And prints submitted for publication need a white border so the editor can make *crop marks* that indicate what part of the photo is to be used.

Be sure all photos you send to editors are identified. Never write on the picture, and don't use paper clips. Instead, tape a sheet of paper to the back of the photo, with the caption written on the bottom. Don't risk having your captionless photos lost on an editor's desk.

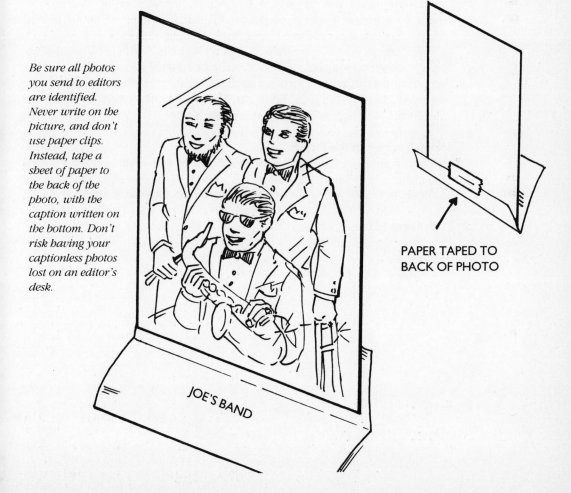

PAPER TAPED TO
BACK OF PHOTO

JOE'S BAND

Photos to be used in your brochure should also be printed *flatter,* if possible, and should be very sharp and clear. You'll probably want to use a close-up, since the picture will be quite small in the brochure. Also, pictures for use in brochures or other publications should have medium grey backgrounds, since pure white and black backgrounds may reproduce poorly when printed.

Sending Photos Through the Post

To send a photograph through the post, you must protect it against the rigours of the post office. Use a reinforced envelope to support the photos. If the pictures are really valuable, stiffen them with extra cardboard and use rubber bands diagonally from corner to corner to hold the material together. Also, though it may be futile, always write or stamp PHOTOS – PLEASE DON'T BEND on the envelope in big red letters.

If you're sending material to an editor for possible use, and you'd like the pictures back, include a stamped addressed envelope (called an *SAE*) and a note asking for their return. Most editors will try to return material to you, but don't send anything you can't afford to lose, because they often get misplaced or damaged in transit. If your pictures run in Thursday's paper, ask about the return of your photos when you make your thank-you call on Friday.

Many papers won't return pictures that are submitted with press releases, so again, don't send valuable material. If you've submitted a story that's accompanied by pictures, there's a good chance that your material will be returned, but don't bet on it. Editors are swamped with pictures, and their desks are always piled high with manuscripts and photos.

Keep Yourself in the Picture

Australian aborigines are right; photographs do capture your spirit – or at least the image of it. Work to get pictures that depict you as you are, and as you want to be seen. Let pictures show your clients and audiences what you're like. Use them to help tell your story. Photos can help you put your best face forward to clients around the country.

CHAPTER EIGHT

DEMO TAPES

The prospective client says, "Okay. Tell me about your music." How do you reply? Can you really describe your music? Can you explain exactly what you do and how you do it? Can you convey the beauty of your performance – in words?

No, you can't. Music is, simply, a unique art that can't be translated into words. You can talk *about* it, sure, and even write about it – but no matter how hard you try, you can't tell people how your music *sounds*.

Other artists don't have this problem. Potters, photographers or carpenters can publicise their craft, and there'll be no uncertainty because you can *see* pottery, pictures and furniture. But when you talk or write about your music, how can you really get the message across?

"Yes, Mr. Jones. We're the best band in town for your party. We play all the standards. Good? Of course we're good. Talented? Absolutely. Our singer even has perfect pitch. What do you mean, 'What do we sound like?' We sound great."

That's the point. You can't tell anyone what you sound like. You can, however, show them – with demonstration tapes.

If your clients are knowledgeable about music – and they rarely will be – or if they will take the recommendation of agents or friends – and they rarely will – you won't need demo tapes. In reality, clients will almost always insist on hearing what they're buying, and you can't really blame them. You'd probably do the same thing if you were hiring a band.

Where Can We Hear You?

Have you heard that one before? You've just finished your sales pitch, you've shown your brochure, press clippings, and letters of recommendation. They're interested in booking you for the annual company dinner-dance. They say, "Everything looks great, and your band is highly recommended. But where can we hear you?"

If you're playing in a club, there's no problem. You just invite them in to hear the band. But if your group plays only private parties, or if you're not currently booked in a club, what do you do? You don't want an entertainment committee to come barging into another client's party, do you?

The answer: demo tapes.

Now, there are two different kinds of demo tapes, made for very different purposes. One is the demo that's intended to sell your band, or a song you've written, to a record company. That kind of demo usually requires extensive production, and involves lots of money and time. In essence, you're making a recording that meets – or exceeds – industry standards, and you'll need a producer, lots of studio time, and perhaps some extra musicians. Such demos are outside the scope of this book, since they aren't really publicity tools but finished products in themselves.

The other kind of demo tape is the one you make to demonstrate what your band can do, and to show what you sound like. Such a tape will show the quality of your music, and the variety of your repertoire – and it has to be good. But it doesn't have to be the same finished, ultra-expensive quality as a tape you're sending to EMI Records. This chapter discusses this second kind of demo – the one that showcases your band, your music, and your wide-ranging performance. It's a sales tool, and a great publicity helper.

Before you start thinking about making a demo, though, think about this: if your demo tape isn't excellent, it will do more harm than good. This doesn't just mean that the music must be good. Good production – and even the finished appearance of the tape – are also important. You won't have to hire a string section or extra percussionists – as you might if you were sending the tape to a record company – but you've got to strive for a really good tape anyway.

The Pros Set The Standard

Everyone today expects excellent, professional-quality recordings because they're accustomed to high-fidelity sound – it's not the exception but the rule. You can buy a portable cassette player for less than fifty pounds that sounds incredibly good, and people are constantly surrounded by well-produced music in cars, homes, offices – even lifts.

Yours has to measure up.

Of course you can use a little cassette recorder to make a demo tape on the job. The drums may be too loud and the vocals will probably be muffled – in fact, the fidelity won't be very good and there'll be noticeable wow and flutter, but it's only a demo tape. Right?

Wrong. When there's well-produced music everywhere, yours has to measure up. Remember, every 30-second commercial features top-quality players, singers, recording and engineering.

When people listen to the radio they hear pop records and commercials that cost a fortune to produce. That's the standard, like it or not, and if your demo falls short – even if the music is terrific – it won't get much consideration.

You've heard the saying, "The medium is the message." That's what's happening here. The quality of the recording, mixing and effects – even the printing of the label – may actually overshadow the musical content. It may not be fair, but that's the way things are. The standards for recorded sound and video are set by the music industry, and those standards apply to your demo just as much as to a pop record.

If you're going to make a demo tape, then, you just have to make it a good one – not spectacular, not over-produced, with layer upon layer of strings and background vocals, but good; it's that simple.

Meet the Competition

What are your competitors – other bands or soloists – doing with their demo tapes? If they aren't using demos, or if their tapes are poor quality, you're in a great position. Yours will automatically be better. But if their tapes are excellent, you'll have to at least match them to compete.

Your clients won't understand the intricacies, expense and effort of spending time in the recording studio. They just know that the demo tape for Band X sounds great, and yours sounds bad. Don't expect them to understand musical or recording ideas or jargon. They won't.

So, for both reasons – industry standards and meeting the competition – you have to commit yourself to producing excellent tapes.

What Do You Need?   Maybe you'll just need a single audio tape to demonstrate your music. Or, you might profit from several specialised tapes, one for each different kind of music you perform.

Perhaps you'll need a demo video to give the full picture. For some performers, a good video will be the most useful publicity tool of all. Cabaret singers, show bands, conductors, soloists, comedians and magicians – who are primarily entertainers – need strong demo videos.

Videos, though, are more expensive to produce, and require much more planning and care. How do you know if it's worth the expense and effort?

If your performance has a strong visual element, you need a video. If costumes, sets or action are important, or if choreography and movement are part of your show, you need a video. If, on the other hand, you just play music, an audio tape or two may be all you need.

Audio Pointers

This book is not a technical manual on making demo tapes; you'll probably rely on professional studio engineers to produce your tape, anyway. Whether you plan to produce your own, or work in a studio, however, these considerations will help you get the best possible tape, at the least possible cost.

Target each tape to an exact audience. If you play pop, jazz, country *and* classical music, your repertoire is exceptionally broad. Will you ever have a client who wants all those different kinds of music? Probably not. When you're in the studio, then, record enough material for as many different tapes as you'll need, and simply package relevant tunes together – pull several tapes, if you need to, from one session.

Don't overestimate a client's flexibility and imagination. If you give her a demo that includes Beethoven when she's looking for Willie Nelson, she'll be suspicious of your country-music abilities. Or if you include sophisticated jazz when a client is planning an eighteenth birthday party for his son, who's into Led Zeppelin and Def Leppard, he'll think you're not the band for his needs – even if you play metal with the best of them. If your musical abilities include different genres, make several tapes. Have a jazz tape, a pop tape, a country demo and a classical one, if you book jobs in all those areas. (In fact, if your abilities really are that extensive, you'll probably need a completely different publicity kit for each specialty.)

Won't that cost a lot? Yes, but the tapes are ultimately sales tools that will help you book jobs. A good demo tape will pay for itself many times over – so in the long run it won't really cost you anything. It will *produce* money.

Be sure to shop around when looking for a studio. Rates vary enormously, and you may be able to save hundreds, or thousands, of pounds by using a smaller studio, rather than the one that's 'hot' at the moment. Don't pay for equipment and expertise that you don't need.

If you're working on a demo tape to sell your songs or group to a record company, you'll probably need to spend lots more money than if you're doing a demo for your band. Where a simple 15-minute band demo might cost £500 (as my last one did), a complete production, with extra musicians, arrangers and all post-production work, could easily cost several thousand. (This will be beyond the reach of many groups; if you're aiming for stardom, you may find that you need financial backers. Be very careful, however, about going into debt to finance your project. If you don't get a record deal, how will that expensive demo ever pay for itself?)

Plan your tape in advance. Think carefully about selections that would appeal to each target audience. Remember, you're not making an album to showcase the music you like – you're making a sales tool for specific groups of clients.

What tunes are requested most often? Which ones always get a positive response? Shouldn't those tunes be on your demo – even if they aren't your personal favourites? Plan your tapes to include a variety, within the musical type, to show what you can do. Perhaps you'll include a couple of standards, a couple of slow tunes, some new material, and some up-tempo numbers.

You won't be able to update the tapes every time a major hit comes out, so try to pick tunes that will last beyond the usual two-week half-life of most pop tunes. You'll have a feeling for the ones that will survive.

When you've decided what to include, do all your rehearsing *before* you get to the studio. Know exactly how each tune will be structured – intro, solos, ending – so you won't waste expensive studio-time making these decisions.

Shop around. Recording studios have sprouted like mushrooms in many communities. Budget *eight-track* and *16-track studios* abound. To find the right studio, it's important to know what you need before you start shopping. Your five-piece rock band will have a hard time producing a good demo in a four-track studio, though of course it's possible. On the other hand, a pianist wouldn't need twenty-four tracks to do a solo tape.

Call some local studios to learn the range of features and cost of services in your area. You can also ask other musicians for recommendations. You'll be surprised at the variety you find – in cost, features and *sound*.

And that's what you're looking for in a studio – a *sound* you like. You shouldn't care whether the studio is trendy cedar, glass and chrome, or even whether it has produced several hit records. You're after a good sound for *your* tape. That's all. Often a studio will be the 'in' place for advertising agencies to produce jingles and commercials, but that doesn't mean it would be the best place to record your demo – and it would probably be very expensive because it's so busy with high-paying ad work.

The best – really the *only* – way to judge a recording studio is by the quality of its products. In searching for a studio, listen to similar work they've done. Do the drums sound right? Is the piano tinny, or full-sounding? Do the instruments have the right timbre? Are they balanced? Are vocals full, with a good, natural sound? Listen critically before you schedule a session, because different studios and engineers have different *sounds*. Part of the difference is the physical set-up, and part is in the intangible mixture of skill, equipment, acoustics and care.

Studios offer a maze of electronic capabilities today, but the same gadgets that can help can also clutter up a take. Be wary of too much equalisation, reverb, compression or stereo separation. You are, after all, making a demo and not a full-fledged album, so don't try to make your four-piece band sound like 12 people. You could have the same problems as some early disco bands whose live performances never matched their recorded work.

So don't overuse – but equally, don't overlook – studio capabilities for augmenting and completing your tape. You can *punch in* to correct mistakes, but don't spend too much time making every single note perfect in every respect. Don't over-produce, in other words, for your audience.

Do you need a full-fledged producer? If you're preparing a demo for a record company, you'll certainly need all the expert help and advice you can get, and a good producer can help with a wide range of decisions, from what tunes to pick to how to mike the drums. If, however, you're doing a demo for your band, your own expertise and a good engineer's knowledge and experience will usually suffice. Talk to the engineer who'll be doing your session in advance, to see if you communicate well, and if you have confidence in his abilities.

Get a firm idea of the price of your demo. What's the cost per hour of recording time? Mixing time? Set-up time? How many tapes are included in the price? If the studio runs out of master tape in the middle of a session, who pays while the engineer re-equalises the recording head?

If you're using an acoustic piano, will it be tuned? If other instruments will be provided – synths, amps, drums – will you be comfortable playing them? If you're using your own outboard equipment, is it good enough for studio use – or is that old volume pedal you use at the club too noisy for recording work?

What about duplicate tapes? How much will the studio charge for a hundred? Are there other duping facilities in town that would provide the same quality for a lot less money? (Probably.) Or, could you do the duping you need yourself? (Again, probably, but listen to a home-made dupe on a good system to be sure there's no *audible wow, flutter* or *distortion*.) Think again about your audience. Would they probably listen to your demo in the car, on a £30 blaster, or on an expensive home stereo system? If you think your demo will usually be played on medium quality equipment, don't waste money on metal tapes and exquisite reproduction.

Expect the session to take longer than it should: they always do. So, expect to pay more than your original estimate. If you can afford it, go ahead and do it right. After all, a poor tape won't create good publicity or book any jobs.

In fact, a poor tape wastes money. Just a little more time spent in punching in to correct one mistake, or adding one overdub, or remixing one more time, might pay for itself with the first job you book.

Consider using a short spoken introduction to present your message to the listener. There's no need to jump immediately into the music.

"Hello. This is Joe, of Joe's Band. Thanks for listening to this demo tape. We've tried to include a representative sample of the hundreds of tunes we know, and we hope you like them."

Some bands even insert commentary between tunes, but it's easy to talk too much. Prospective clients might enjoy the music on your demo enough to listen over and over again, but they probably wouldn't put up with a continuing sales pitch. Keep any introductory material short.

Finish your demo tapes so they look fully professional. You know by now that appearance is often as important as content, so make your tapes look good by using printed labels and inserts.

Of course, you can just type a label and stick it on the tape, but that doesn't look like a successful musician, does it? Any quick-copy printer can provide custom-printed cassette labels in any colour. Just prepare the camera-ready art exactly as you did for your letterhead, and the printer will do the rest.

You'll probably also want cardboard inserts to fit inside the plastic cassette boxes in addition to the labels you've stuck on the tapes. Again, your printer can prepare them for you, and you can do the artwork yourself, or have a typesetter prepare it inexpensively. The insert does the same job for a tape that the album cover does for a record, so make yours look good.

If you work through agents, and most musicians do, don't put your address or phone number on the tapes or inserts, because agents don't want their clients contacting you directly. Your name, logo and the tape contents are enough. (When booking jobs yourself, simply include your business card.)

The Gibson/ Bennett band uses a less expensive, simple-to-produce black-and-white insert that any printer can provide. (The printer will 'score' the cardboard so it will bend in the right places for an exact fit.)

THE GIBSON/BENNETT BAND

The Look of Love (Introduction) ■ Memory (from "Cats") ■ Be Young, Be Foolish, Be Happy ■ Saving All My Love for You ■ Living in America ■ Sentimental Journey ■ Old Time Rock and Roll ■ New York, New York ■ Boogie-Woogie Bugle Boy ■ Shout

THE Gibson/Bennett BAND

MUSIC FOR EVERYBODY

Records

Can you use records as demos? It's possible, of course, but it's rarely done because records are expensive in small quantities, they're impossible to update, and producing a good-looking album is complicated. Also, records are losing popularity – compact discs and digital audio tape are the future of recorded sound.

If you do shows or concerts, however, you might need records as an after-show sales item, even though producing a record is a very expensive project. If you choose to do an album, spend plenty of time and money on the cover, both front and back; make it look as good as any record in a shop (even though four-colour photography, design and printing are very expensive). Remember, the medium is the message, and a cheap-looking black-and-white record jacket will be counter-productive.

Flexible *soundsheets* are a compromise medium. These plastic sheets can be sent by post inexpensively, and sound adequate. They don't require expensive covers, either, and if you're looking for an unusual medium to publicise your music, and you need lots of copies, soundsheets may be a good investment. However, they're much more expensive to produce than a few dozen cassette tapes.

Using Audio Tapes

Your aim is to publicise your music, so don't be stingy with your tapes. If you buy wisely, you can keep the unit cost surprisingly low. Shop around, and order as many tapes as you think you can use. Although budget is a consideration, 25 tapes would be a good number to start with.

Demo tapes are like seed. If you put out enough, you'll reap a full crop of bookings. So why ask for demo tapes to be returned? Encourage people to keep them. "No, Mrs. Jones, we don't need that tape back. We hope you'll keep it in your car and play it for your friends. We know it will remind you of all the fun you had at your company Christmas party."

Keep enough tapes on hand to distribute as requests come in. Send them out the same day. A stack of demo tapes on your shelf won't do you any good at all.

Video Demos

Do you need a pop-style video? Probably not. (If you do, this isn't the book for you.) Industry estimates on the cost of a 'video' start around ten thousand pounds, and go up to over a hundred. If you can afford that much money for one tune, you're already a success.

Maybe you are trying to make it with a record, and you feel a video will ensure the record's success. Work with your record company, or backers, to get funding for the video, and search for the right producer.

This chapter, however, is about *demos*, not fully-fledged promo videos.

Do you need a video to promote your music? You do if:

● You produce a *show* that's booked as entertainment.
● There is a strong *visual* element in what you do.
● You are exceptionally *telegenic* and know how to use the medium.
● You are *frequently on television,* and have already acquired impressive clips of your appearances.

Not every musician and band will profit from a video demo. You may not need one if you just play music. If yours is a dance or club band, there may not be a strong visual element, telegenic personality, or charisma. (That's not necessarily bad, of course. Many musicians are musicians first, and performers second. They like to play music, and don't think of themselves as 'entertainers' at all.)

If your band makes frequent changes in personnel, a video would also be a bad idea. A client can't tell what you look like from an audio demo, but if he *sees* that your singer is blonde and trim, he may be unhappy if the singer on *his* job is brunette and overweight. A video can lock your personnel decisions in place – and clients can be very unhappy, and feel cheated, if they don't get what they've seen.

Obviously, if you don't have the money for a well-produced demo video, just rely on your audio tape. A poor video is like a poor violinist – any lack of quality is immediately apparent.

Finding a Producer

Shop around. This is even more important with video than with audio. There's division in the video production world between *commercial* and *consumer quality* video equipment and production. With new equipment and digital techniques, however, this distinction may be less important in the future.

Commercial video producers work mostly for businesses and advertising agencies. They use larger tape and better, much more expensive, equipment. They produce video training materials and commercials, and they're often accustomed to big budgets.

If you ask a commercial video producer for a quote on a 12-minute demo tape, you might be told that a minimum price would be five thousand pounds. That's a lot of money.

Consumer-level producers are the people you see videotaping weddings. They use essentially the same cameras and equipment that you may have at home, and charge much less for their work. They'll usually work directly in the VHS format. Often, the quality of their work isn't as good as that of commercial producers, and they may not have the same technical capabilities – but these drawbacks may not be relevant.

One new development that may change the video production scene is the use of advanced personal computer programmes in video editing. Sophisticated programmes give advanced capabilities to home equipment, and if your producer uses this route he may be able to provide superior – perhaps even digital – quality at consumer prices, and with consumer equipment. This field is changing so quickly that you'll have to check out the situation in your area when you start looking for a producer.

For budget reasons, you'll probably work with a *consumer-level* producer, but if you're careful, you can still get an excellent video for much less than a commercial producer would have to charge. Use the Yellow Pages; look for someone who's done band demos before, and spend time talking, looking, listening and asking questions before you make a commitment. Look at the producer's samples very carefully. Notice image quality, colour, *video noise* (flecks, spots, bands on the screen). Does the colour balance change from shot to shot? Are the fades even? Are the cuts clean – and logical? What kind of lighting does this producer typically use? Direct frontal spotlights that make people look like they're being interrogated? Usually such *light-on-the-camera* techniques are the mark of an amateur.

Find out how he would shoot your group, and pay special attention to his audio technique and equipment. How many mikes would he use? What kind of mixer? Listen critically to his samples for balance, tone, wow and flutter, and crispness. If possible, listen through a good pair of headphones, or at least on a high-quality stereo system. Don't rely on the built-in speakers in a TV set to make this important judgement. What happens to the soundtrack when the picture changes? Is there distortion or poor balance?

What about the ideas, the logical movement from point to point? Does this producer use enough cameras to do close-ups at the right time in your performance? Is his sense of timing good – or do some shots seem too long and others too short? Are the titles imaginative, or staid and boring? Remember, your audience is accustomed to the best.

These are hard questions, but you must be satisfied about them before you start on your own video. You're about to commit a chunk of money, and a lot of time, so be convinced that you'll get a tape that will work hard for you – a useful sales tool that will *make*, not *cost,* money.

Video Bits

Knowing what you'll need will help you decide which producer to hire. To repeat, this isn't a book on producing videos – which is a complex and rapidly changing subject – but these important considerations will help.

Use the free media university we've discussed. Television brings the best output of the best producers and engineers into your home every day. Watch their products closely, because the same techniques that work for them will work for you. You'll write, or at least work on, your own script, so you should know what 'works' on TV, and what looks good. If the average time a shot is on the screen is six seconds, don't plan to include a 30-second one in your script – it will seem catatonic.

Pay particular attention to commercials, because that's where the big production money is spent. A good 30-second commercial is like a well-done short story and can be a masterpiece of video art. Think of commercials as little demos, and watch how they get their message across.

Keep a written record of the average length of their shots – usually three to five seconds – and the proportion of close-ups to long shots. Watch their titles, and listen to how they use the music. A 30-second commercial may cost well over twenty-five thousand pounds to produce, so you can be sure that you're studying the best efforts of the best professionals in the business.

Audio quality is crucial. After all, your video is about music. Most video producers work with voice only, or with pre-recorded music, so you'll have to investigate their audio recording capabilities.

A good video demo will require extreme care in recording your sound. One mike on the camera won't do the job. Neither will two mikes plugged into the tape unit. If you're taping live, work with a full board and as many mikes as you need. Be sure the mix is what you like before it's put on tape, because, depending on the route you choose, you may not have a chance to remix later.

One possibility is to use the audio demo you've already recorded, and lip-synch as you shoot the video. This must be done *perfectly*, however, or it will look sloppy – or silly. Adding video to an existing audio tape is possible, but it's tedious and risky.

Shooting live requires a script. Work with the producer to sketch out, or *story-board*, exactly how each song will be photographed. How many seconds on the keyboard for the introduction? When will he cut to the drums for an elaborate fill? What about fading to the backing singers for their *Do-Wops?* This requires planning and time, and isn't cheap. You should, of course, know as much as possible about what you want going into the project, but you should also work on the script with the producer, and be open to suggestions about flow, pacing and technical matters. After all, he's the expert.

Learn which video techniques your producer can use, and be familiar with what they mean. *Long shots, close-ups, pans, wipes, freeze-frames, cuts, fades, superimpositions* and *computer-generated graphics* will give your video a professional look. But they must be planned and coordinated – they won't just happen.

If several cameras are being used, the producer will use *SMPTE (Society of Motion Picture and Television Engineers)* code to keep all the images and music coordinated. This is a complex procedure that keeps the music and video from each camera and recording device in perfect synch. Small producers may not have this capability – so be sure to view samples of similar work before you sign up.

Titles and artwork are important. Find out what's available, and how much it costs. Look at the computer-generated graphics possibilities, and see what would fit your music. If you're a classical pianist, a high-tech, whirling, phantasmagoric title probably wouldn't be appropriate, no matter how exciting the technique is.

Should you incorporate your logo in the title? Why not? It represents your music and you, and should be part of all your publicity material. You can also use collages of printed material, close-ups of reviews, and other elements to give your demo a 'story' feel. Such still shots, however, must be carefully scripted to maintain pace and continuity.

Use TV clips. If you have good clips of previous television appearances, work them into your tape. In fact, if you have several good clips, particularly if you've been on prestigious shows, your demo might include nothing more than those clips strung together.

Each time you perform on TV, get a tape of your appearance. Ask the station for a copy (you provide the tape and make arrangements for copying in advance), and also get a friend to record a back-up tape off the air. Don't miss such opportunities for free, professionally produced publicity.

Your video can also include clips from concerts, interviews, or even shots from several performances. Do you have a tape of hundreds of people dancing to your band's 'Louie, Louie'? Use it. Even if the video isn't perfect, the impact will be strong.

Quality does count. Can't you just use a quick-and-dirty tape that's made at the show, with a consumer-quality camera, and no editing? Can't you just get a friend in to videotape your band on the spot? Of course. You can use anything – but remember that if the quality of the production is poor, the publicity results will be, too.

Get it in writing. Video producers usually charge by the job. Discuss price in detail, and be sure that you understand exactly what you're getting. To be safe, insist on a written contract with your producer. Spell out exactly what you expect to receive, when it will be finished, and how much it will cost. This doesn't imply that you don't trust him – it can simply avoid unpleasantness and confusion later.

Don't be a copy-cat. Each time a videotape is copied, the quality of the duplicate degenerates considerably. And a copy of a copy – which is what you'll usually give to clients, can suffer from video noise, poor picture quality, inaccurate colour, and poor audio. That's one reason professional producers use larger formats – there's more room on the tape for signal, and each copy loses proportionately less quality.

You probably won't be able to make your own video copies, and the ones you buy will cost much more than audio demos. Check with your producer for his duplication prices, and call the video services companies in the Yellow Pages for comparison. Insist that the copies you get are as good as they can be, and work to attain a tape you'll be proud to watch.

Using Video Tapes

Since videotapes are expensive, you won't blanket the area with them the way you do with audio demos. But if you've gone to the trouble of producing a good video, be sure that all your prime clients have copies.

All the agents who book your music should certainly have their copies, and you should keep a few available for your own clients to view. It's appropriate, however, to ask that a videotape be returned, and to keep track of who has your tapes. Enclose an SAE to help ensure that your copies get back to you. To get the most impact from your video, prepare a client for what the tape contains. If you especially like one aspect, tell the viewer about it before he's seen the tape. "When you watch our demo, Mr. Jones, notice the crowd reaction to our music. We really work with the audience to get a party going, and this video shows it."

This way, Mr. Jones is alerted to watch for your strong point – you've made the point twice, by telling and then showing, which doesn't hurt your chances.

Use videos when you have a message that should be seen as well as heard. Use them wisely, however, and don't be bedazzled with the chance to 'be on TV.' It won't do you any good to be on the tube if your appearance isn't up to television's standards. If you have an act with a strong visual component and if you can produce a good demo video, however, it could become the most-used publicity tool in your kit.

After all, if video messages sell everything from soap powder to cars, why shouldn't they sell your music?

CHAPTER NINE

FINDING PROFESSIONAL HELP

In your battle to get noticed, we've said that you, yourself, can produce almost everything you'll need – and you can. With patience, a few graphic skills, some basic tools, and the nuts-and-bolts information from earlier chapters in this book, you'll have what you need to do it yourself.

But perhaps you don't think you have any artistic ability, or you don't have the patience for tedious layout chores. Maybe you're paralysed by 'writer's block' every time you face a typewriter. Possibly you just don't have time to plan your own publicity. Perhaps you even have enough money to hire all the professional help you need. Actually, you'll probably use professionals for some publicity projects and do other tasks yourself. This chapter will direct you to the expert assistance you need.

In seeking professional help, shop around. Use the guidelines in this chapter, and get several *specific, written* quotes from different people. Prices will vary considerably – but quality can, too. Spend your money wisely, and you'll get extra mileage from every pound you spend on publicity.

How Good Are They?
One of the most frustrating aspects of 'creative' businesses is that anyone can call himself a professional. Buy a guitar, learn a few chords, and hey presto! – you're a musician. Anyone with a couple of cameras and some lights can refer to himself as a professional photographer, and anyone with a drawing board, some rulers and coloured pencils is a commercial artist.

How do you separate the good from the bad? How do you find someone who is technically excellent, understands your needs, is truly creative – and affordable? Should you try to save money by hiring a beginner or part-timer, or use established professionals?

This chapter gives rough ideas of what professionals charge for their services, though rates vary so much that you must check each one in your own area. If a designer would charge £100 to design your brochure, you may decide to learn how to do your own paste-up and layout. If a photographer would charge £250 to shoot two rolls of film, you may decide to spend an afternoon with your own 35mm camera, and do your own pictures.

If you decide to do most of these publicity chores yourself, you'll save money, but the quality may not be up to professional standards – and you may take forever to finish a project. However, you are a creative person, so if you have time and patience, why not do it yourself? It may take time, and some tasks (layout and paste-up, for example) are tedious and require patience, but with a little practice you can do a good job.

On the other hand, if you get professional assistance you'll pay for it, but you'll have the benefit of the person's training, experience and creativity. And since you're paying for it, you can insist that it be finished on time.

How To Find Help

How do you locate competent designers, copy writers and photographers? You could choose at random from the Yellow Pages, but there are better ways to find the right person for you. Start by asking for recommendations. When you see good examples of similar work, find out who produced them. The key word is *similar*. Don't expect an excellent wedding photographer to automatically produce the head shots you need, or a fashion illustrator to be an expert at logo design. Professionals usually specialise.

Also check at local colleges, polytechnics and private art schools. Students won't have years of experience, but they may have a fresh approach, a lot of enthusiasm – and be reasonably priced.

Freelancers and moonlighting professionals offer excellent possibilities. Often designers, writers, typesetters and photographers who work during the day for businesses, universities or government, do freelance work on the side. Call the advertising, public relations or publications departments of these institutions and ask if anyone is available for outside work. Also check at camera shops and printers.

Full-time, established professionals are always available, and may offer the best value – though they may be more expensive. Again, be sure that their specialities match your needs, because professionals often work in very narrow areas of expertise. Technical writers may not be able to prepare a good press release. Architectural photographers may not know how to light a group photo. The Yellow Pages will direct you to professional help, but don't be awed by a fancy office; look for samples that match your needs.

And don't forget to shop around. Never take the first person who's available, because you have nothing with which to compare his or her skills. Prices vary, and so does creativity. Paying more doesn't automatically guarantee the best quality – but it might.

Once you've found several possibilities, how can you assess the publicity professionals in your area to be sure you get exactly what you need? Consider:

1. *Do you communicate well with the person?* Do you like him or her? Do they understand what you want? Do you think they'll spend time working with you? Or are they condescending, rushed, perfunctory? Too busy with their own work to take time with your small project?
2. *Look at samples of similar work.* Artists, photographers and writers all have portfolios of their best work, and they'll be happy to show them to you – you may even get some ideas from what they've done. Compare apples with apples, however; if you're looking for help with layout, be sure to see samples of brochures or letterheads that match your needs. In every area, look for quality, for precision. Does this person take pride in his work?
3. *Ask for written cost estimates*, and be sure everything is included. Don't be afraid to ask, or you may be unpleasantly surprised. Does the cost include materials? Are there any hidden expenses such as outside, subcontracted costs

that will be extra? Be sure you get the bottom-line total. People who work in advertising often enjoy nearly unlimited budgets, so let them know that you're concerned about cost – but don't be petty. It's easy to be too cheap, and end up wasting your money by going second (or third) class.

4. *Will the work be delivered when it's promised?* Can you depend on it? Does this person have a good reputation for reliability? If you're counting on a photographer who only freelances at weekends, are you sure your pictures will be ready when you need them? You usually won't have a contract, so if you're especially concerned about deadlines, ask for, and check with, past references.

5. *Who will own the material that's produced?* Always discuss this point, because it can be important. Most photographers will keep the negatives, even though you paid for the materials – that's the custom in photography. On the other hand, artists will usually give you the original artwork, but to be certain, you should ask.

If you're like most musicians, you won't have a lot of extra money to spend producing publicity, so do a little research to be sure that the help you get will fit your budget.

The Professionals Are There – If You Need Them
In planning your publicity, here are some of the professionals who are available to help you. You may not need them now, but you might call on them later as your publicity programme grows.

Public relations firms are the ultimate professionals in the business of getting noticed, but they're probably too expensive for most musicians. These are the people who produce PR campaigns for businesses, government agencies and celebrities. Much of their time is spent *networking*. They are responsible for producing press releases, stories, brochures and photographs, and for placing ideas with the media – 'getting good press.' Public relations firms also plan and produce all kinds of special events to create media attention – new-product introductions, press conferences, parties, contests and so on.

If you become a star, you'll need to retain a PR consultant to 'pump the press' and keep your name in print, or if you are working on a special project with a sizable budget – a local music festival, for example – you might want to work with a pro.

For most musicians, public relations firms would be a good choice for publicising a specific project, such as an album release or a concert series – where a special budget would be devised. PR people can handle as little or as much of your publicity as you can afford.

Public relations professionals commonly charge a weekly or monthly retainer fee that could be anything from £500 to £5,000 a month for public relations services. You'll find these firms in the Yellow Pages under "Public relations consultants."

Visit a couple of PR firms – the smaller ones would be the best bet – and explain your publicity goals. Find out what they could do for you, and how much they would charge. If they are even close to your budget, ask for a written proposal in which they'll outline exactly what they would do for you, and what their fee would be. Even if you can't afford their help, you'll have the pleasure of knowing what your own publicity efforts are worth in pounds and pence, and you may pick up some good ideas.

Finding a copywriter to help with your brochures, press releases and feature stories might be more difficult than you'd think. There are as many different kinds of writing as there are kinds of music, and you need a style that matches your specific publicity projects.

At first, you may think of an English teacher as a writing expert. Actually, freelance copywriters and editors will be more appropriate for your needs, because your writing will be closer to advertising than to an English essay. Teachers or students of journalism, however, might be worth checking out.

Call newspapers, magazines, ad agencies and public relations firms to get leads on good freelance writers. You'll pay by the hour or by the project; again, don't hesitate to talk about money. You don't know how fast a writer will work, and you don't want to owe £100 for a one-page brochure when you were expecting a £25 fee. Writers' fees vary considerably, so ask before you commit yourself; a professional copywriter might charge in excess of £20 per hour.

Ask to see samples of similar work. Don't assume that just because a writer has excellent command of the English language she'll do a good job on your brochure. You have to make sure that she knows what you want and can produce it.

Artists, like writers, develop narrow specialities. You need a graphic designer to help with logo and brochure design and layout chores. Fine art is something else – a great painter may have no idea how to prepare a PMT for the printer, so don't ask your neighbour who paints landscapes to help with your letterhead.

Always examine examples of similar work, and judge it by what you need. Does it look stilted, old fashioned? Are the details correct? Does the piece look fresh, creative, or does it have a tired, institutional appearance? The greatest artist in the world won't help you if he's not appropriate.

You can get names of designers from the same sources that recommend writers, and from typesetters and art-supply shops. Students can produce excellent work, and their rates should be lower to match their lack of experience.

Photographers, like musicians, vary greatly in experience, skill and competence. Photography can be fine art or a mundane craft, and you'll do best if you can find someone in between these extremes. You don't want avant-garde weirdness (unless you're a weird, avant-garde band), but neither do you want the kind of photographer who nails his lights to the floor and shoots each portrait exactly the same way.

Look for someone whose work suits your needs. Ask to see samples of group and head shots. Look for posing – is it natural or stiff? Look at the backgrounds – are they the same in every picture, or does the photographer vary location with each subject? Look at the photos technically – is the focus crisp and sharp? Is there a good tonal range from white to black? Are there spots, flecks, black dots on the picture? In photography, cleanliness is next to Godliness, so look around the studio for signs of carelessness and sloppiness.

Finding the right photographer may be as simple as asking around. Look at brochures and publicity photos used by your competition. Some photographers attempt to 'do it all', but many are highly specialised. Look for a photographer who shoots models and bands, and who likes the creative challenge of matching his photos to your image and moods. Some photographers charge by the hour, not including materials. Others quote a set price for a session (probably three hours), including a certain number of prints. Most will provide you with contact sheets, and you'll select the prints you like for a per-print fee. The best, and most common, procedure, is for the photographer to print one or two of the shots you like and have them duplicated inexpensively at a mass production house. The photographer will expect this, because he can't even buy photographic paper at a price that's competitive with the mass production houses. Remember, though, that photographers retain ownership of the negatives, even though you may have paid for the film.

What if you find a terrific graphic artist, but you can't afford his work rates? Why not swap your music for his art? *Bartering* can benefit both parties. In bartering, swap value for value, and don't reduce the quality of what you offer or receive. A photographer might swap two photo sessions and 10 prints in exchange for your band playing for his party. Or a writer whose daughter is planning a wedding may write your brochure and several press releases in exchange for your string quartet's playing at the wedding reception. If the idea appeals to you, be sure to ask. You may be surprised at the deals you can make.

All these publicity experts are available to help you. They know their crafts, and can give you the benefit of years of experience. Successful people often delegate specific tasks to others, and you may prefer to have someone else prepare your publicity material to free your time for other projects. All you have to do is ask – and pay.

Remember, even the best writers, photographers and artists can't read your mind; it's your responsibility to let them know what you want. Show samples, keep cuttings files of similar work, ask questions, draw sketches. The professional you are hiring wants to please you by providing what you're seeking, so be as clear as you can about what you want and can afford.

Never allow yourself to be awed by technical vocabulary or jargon from another discipline. There is no reason that you should know the language of printing, photography or professional public relations. Those people probably don't know music terms either, so ask questions to find out what you need to know. If the person you've hired won't answer your questions clearly, find someone else.

Once more, with feeling: do as much of your own publicity work as possible; after all, you're the one who benefits from all this effort. You may be able to produce almost everything, but don't skimp to the point that the quality suffers. Don't do yourself out of a quality job by insisting on the cheapest everything, every time. A few more rolls of film, a better grade of paper, may add just a little to your overall costs but result in the superior quality that you need.

PART TWO

USING YOUR
PUBLICITY TOOLS
TO GET NOTICED

CHAPTER TEN

PUBLICITY AND
THE MEDIA

Now you've prepared the tools you need – letterheads, business cards, photos and demo tapes. How do you use them to attract clients and audiences?

We'll explore lots of ways – from special events to T-shirts, but we'll start with the biggest fish in the publicity pond – the *media*. We'll see how individual musicians and unknown performers can catch the media's interest – by using publicity hooks. News stories, feature articles, regular calendar listings, and mention in columns will combine to raise your visibility to new heights.

The Media   Actually, there is no such thing as *the media*. Instead, there are thousands of different media, large and small, local and national. *The media* includes both the BBC and a small independent radio station. It includes *The Economist* and the free paper distributed around your neighbourhood. It includes *The Guardian* and the *Stockport Messenger*.

Still, people speak of the media as though it were an imposing monolith and anyone would be afraid to approach such a powerful institution. Fortunately, the media isn't really overwhelming at all.

To begin with, think of the media as being local writers, artists, photographers, technicians and business-people who together make up newspapers, radio and TV stations, magazines and other communications outlets in your community. When you approach a media person, it won't be a national celebrity; it will be someone from your community *who needs your story as much as you need his help*.

Hard to believe? It's true.

Media people need you because they need your ideas. They need news and features to interest their readers and viewers. Every day, editors face the same challenge – to fill up all that blank space, all that empty air-time. If your story ideas are interesting, you'll be welcomed.

But you do have to know the basic principles.

1. First, learn to recognise trends.
2. Learn what makes a good feature story.
3. Learn to think like a publicist who recognises *news pegs* and *feature hooks* everywhere.
4. Learn to relate your music and performance to broader issues that appeal to the public.
5. Finally, learn to reach media people by using press releases to generate news and feature stories. Your release could simply give them the idea for a story, or you might write and photograph it yourself.

We'll talk about newspapers and broadcast outlets in more detail later, but first – what makes news?

What's News

News tells what's happening in the world that's important and interesting, in the opinion of an editor. This includes, certainly, items of national and international interest, but it also involves local events that are important to you and your career.

Music is not usually a 'hard news' area, so most of your media exposure will probably be through feature stories that focus on interesting facets of your performance and life. There will be times, though, when you'll make news, so you should recognise what's newsworthy.

News stories answer the readers' questions and, traditionally, tell "who, what, when, where, why and how." (This simple formula is a useful way to remember what's important in news stories – think of it as the *five w's and an h*.)

Every day, editors must decide what to cover, to print or to broadcast, because there isn't room for everything. To help make these decisions, editors ask:

- Is it important?
- Is it interesting?
- Does it appeal to our audience?
- Does it pass the 'who cares?' or 'so what?' test?

News stories should be factual, with no opinions expressed. They give just the facts, and deliver them in a particular style, sometimes called the *inverted pyramid*. News-writing is discussed in the next chapter, but basically, a news story always starts with the most important facts and adds explanations and details later.

Watch your local paper for *news* items that affect the music world, and clip them for your file. (This doesn't include 'news' stories that were obviously created to keep famous stars' names in the news. You probably won't need to make news by hitting a photographer or suing *The Sun*.)

Often, music does tie in with *news stories*. For example:

In a budget-tightening move, the local education authority votes to cut funding for instrumental music tuition. That's news. You're an instrumental teacher and your job is at stake. You must use the media to convince the community and education authority that music education is important.

There has been an outcry in national and local papers about sexually explicit rock lyrics. You, as a rock musician, write an editorial for the newspaper, appear on a radio chat show, and address a meeting of local parents and teachers to explain your band's position on this issue. Even if your band isn't directly affected, you have gained some recognition by connecting yourself with a live media topic.

Your city council is mounting a campaign to promote the city's image to private investors. As part of this campaign, they hold a contest to choose a theme song for their TV and radio sales extravaganza. You get several stories in the paper and TV news, and lots of air-play for the winning song. You have taken advantage of the city's interest in economic salesmanship and linked yourself directly to it.

Your piano studio is so successful that you are able to design and build a new facility that incorporates a recital hall, private classrooms, a library and computer teaching aids. You should tie into news stories on teaching (always a popular news issue), entrepreneurs, building design and computers.

There are dozens of news issues that affect musicians. When you link yourself, your music, or your group to these issues, you automatically expand your influence.

In practice, you'll find that there is a continuum – a range of story ideas, with news on one end, and features on the other. Most stories about the arts fall somewhere between the two extremes – there may be an element of news, but focus is usually on a human interest angle. Don't waste time trying to decide whether a story is news or feature – it's probably both.

Feature This

Though you'll try to be newsworthy, you'll probably find it easier to get media attention through *feature stories* that focus on people and interesting activities. Features are written to entertain as well as enlighten, and almost always are in a more interesting, subjective, relaxed style than a news story would be. Sometimes feature articles include interviews, often they incorporate photographs, and they're frequently longer than news stories.

In many newspapers, the first section is devoted mostly to news, but the rest of the paper is filled with features – the local section, life-style pages, arts review, business events, and even the sports pages include articles on interesting people and happenings. This is where most of your newspaper exposure will be.

You can't just call an editor and say, "Hi. My name's Joe, and I play the guitar in a rock band. How about doing a story on me?" That's not the way it works. You've got to have an *angle*.

What's an angle? It's a mathematical description of a hook. Find an approach that ties your music in with something bigger, that's of interest to lots of people. Link yourself with a trend, a fad, a worthwhile project or a news story, and try again.

"Hi, Mr. Editor. My name's Joe, and I play guitar in a band that's giving a series of free workshops at inner-city high schools. We're working with young musicians, helping them learn about the music business. Our first session was standing-room-only, and we thought you might like to send a writer and photographer to the next event."

That's a lot better. It's more likely to arouse an editor's curiosity, because you're doing something that involves the community. It's really interesting, and the editor knows you have something to offer.

There are *trends* in news and feature stories. From year to year, different subjects catch the attention of the public and of editors, and as a result, the amount of newspaper space devoted to different issues changes over time. One month there are lots of articles on smoking and health; another month you'll see lots of pieces on jogging and health instead. News, like everything else, is subject to the pressures of changing fashion.

So learn to recognise trends. Read newspapers and magazines. When you see a new fad emerging – aerobic exercise, for example, or jogging, or walking – figure out how to relate your musical activities to this new interest. Maybe one percent of newspaper readers are interested in the trumpet, while 50 percent of them are interested in health issues. Your challenge as a trumpet player is to find a way to link trumpet playing with the health issues of the day. Can you do it? Of course.

Or perhaps you'd like to tie your music to another subject that interests lots of people – education, say. What if you're not a teacher; can you still link your projects to learning? Of course. Did you enter the computer age so you could MIDI your synthesiser to a computer? Have you developed a unique method of teaching rock guitar that you've successfully used with 30 students? Did you write and record several simple songs that your school-teacher spouse uses in elementary classes? Did you learn to play the bass, even though you started professional life as a trumpet player, because there's more work for bassists? These ideas all link easily with the idea of learning, education, personal advancement. They could be developed into hooks for stories that would grab readers' attention – about computers, teaching, elementary education, or self-education.

Publicity Practice

Make a list of news and feature themes that are 'current' right now. What fascinates the media this month? Computers? Health? Nutrition? Poverty? Self-development, reaching one's fullest potential? New businesses? Entrepreneurs? Women in new roles? High technology?

First, list subjects that you see over and over again on TV features and in newspapers and magazines – call it your *What's Current* list. Then brainstorm ways your music could relate – even if it's only a slight connection. Writers and editors, more than most people, are interested in what captures the public's interest, and if you can tie into a popular issue, you'll find yourself featured.

As usual in brainstorming, be as creative as possible. If your ideas won't work, that's fine – but maybe they will. For example, does the press seem fascinated by smoking and health? How could you relate your music to this issue? A few ideas:

- If you work in nightclubs, do a story on how you cope with smokiness in the room. Say how you go outside and do deep-breathing exercises for 10 minutes after each job to clear your lungs of smoke. Talk about how you hang your clothes in the garage so your wardrobe won't smell like a nightclub. Discuss what your doctor has told you about breathing that smoke-filled air every night for years – is it equivalent to smoking a pack of cigarettes a day? More? What can non-smoking nightclub patrons learn from your experience?
- If you run a youth band, invite a lung specialist to speak to your students, demonstrating the loss of lung capacity that comes with smoking. Relate this to wind instrument playing. Perhaps your band could take the lead in a national youth/school 'stamp out smoking' campaign.

● If you're a pianist in a bar, try for a feature called 'Smoke Gets in My Eyes.' Discuss how difficult it is to sing with customers blowing smoke in your face, and how difficult it is to avoid the problem without offending them. Talk about the ever-present cigarette burns on the club's grand piano. Point out the times your clothes have been ruined by careless smokers. Show how smokiness irritates your contact lenses.

Do these ideas seem far-fetched? Perhaps, but this is the kind of thing that editors and writers love – a *peg* on which they can hang their stories, an *angle* that allows them to focus on something that links up with a larger trend. Try it. You'll be surprised at how you can fit your music into a larger issue.

What's The Angle, Where's The Hook?

You see now that the *hook* is important – it snares readers' interest. When you start thinking like a publicist, you realise that not only do you have to hook the reader, but to reach that reader you first have to hook the editor. It helps to know what editors do and what they like.

Editors are the first step in the story-selection process. They determine what gets covered and how much time or space it gets. They're under immense pressure from all sides, and have to decide which stories to run, which ones to leave out. Sometimes they may run a story as a favour to a friend, but usually editors choose stories to interest readers or viewers. Their ultimate aim, of course, is to sell newspapers or attract viewers – and sell more ads.

So, when you call and say, "Hi, Mr. Editor. My name's Joe, I play guitar in a rock band, and we'd like to have a feature story on us," your chances of success are zero. You haven't passed the 'so what?' test. The editor doesn't see anything interesting in the fact that you're a guitar player – even a good guitar player. You haven't found a hook.

Return to your cuttings file to see what kinds of stories newspapers in your area typically run about musicians, artists and community groups. Are most stories related to concerts and recitals? Or do they frequently run profiles of successful people who have overcome obstacles? Are most of their music-related features community oriented? Do they like new ideas, fads, technology?

Read those stories carefully, because yours will take the same approach. Strange as it may seem, writers and editors are quite conservative, and once they find a story formula that works they'll stick with it. You'll improve your chances for coverage if you fit into their story schemes.

Thus, if most articles about musicians in your local paper emphasise their community involvement, go out and get involved – and you'll get noticed. If, on the other hand, the music stories are mostly reviews, invite the reviewer to your next performance, with plenty of material sent to her beforehand to acquaint her with your music. Go with the flow; don't try to start a new media wave by yourself.

Plan Ahead

Once your publicity wagon starts rolling, you'll find that it's easier and easier to get noticed. But you have to plan carefully. Newspapers and magazines operate on a rigid deadline schedule that can't be changed just because you didn't know about it – or you forgot. If you're publicising a big event, you'll need to plan months ahead to get all the publicity you need.

Call the publications and broadcast stations you're interested in. Ask about deadlines, including the listings sections, regular columns, and news and feature stories. Tell them what you're planning and find out who the appropriate editors are, who does the theatre and music reviews, and whether photographers are available. You may have to talk to several departments, but you'll have the information you need to get your information to the right person, and in time to be used.

To help remember deadlines, you could create a master deadline calendar or chart, showing exactly when each media outlet needs certain information. Perhaps a simple list on your noticeboard will suffice: "Monday – mid-week newspaper listings and Sunday feature articles, Wednesday – Saturday Leisure Guide, Thursday – Sunday events directory," and so on. Make it clear, so you won't miss good publicity because you forgot a deadline.

Let's take a really big project – publicity for an amateur orchestra/theatre's musical comedy production – as an example to see how much free publicity we could produce. In a case like this, you'd have a committee of assistants because there's lots of work involved. (Of course, the chances are that you'll never be in charge of publicity for such a theatrical production, but whatever your musical project may be, you can use some of these same techniques. You may only need one or two of these ideas for your band – but you might need them all.)

First, state the publicity goals for yourself, your organisation, your committee. Write them down. "Our goals in publicising this performance of *Money Talks* are to increase the attendance at all three performances, raise community awareness of our theatrical company and orchestra, focus attention on our talent, make fund-raising and ticket-selling jobs easier, and add good publicity cuttings to our files." Be sure that everyone involved knows the importance of good publicity in reaching these goals.

Use your wall calendar and datebook to sketch out when your main publicity thrusts must happen. Remember, deadlines won't wait and excuses don't count. If your news release doesn't arrive on time, your event won't be mentioned. Even small papers and radio stations are flooded with promotion for worthy events.

Here's a rough sketch of one way to publicise the musical comedy your school or amateur group is producing. The steps would be much the same, though probably on a smaller scale, for a nightclub band, a concert, recital or almost any other musical event. Remember, these are just suggestions. You don't have to do them all; in fact, you might not need any of them, so don't feel overwhelmed by the possibilities or the amount of work involved. If your musical activity is a rock band playing the club circuit, you'll devise a quite different, but still important, list of ways to publicise your group.

1. *The big day*. As soon as the date is chosen, announce it to all your contacts. Write a short press release and send it to all feature editors, reviewers, other theatre groups, community leaders, and newsletter publishers who might mention your activity. Early mention should help 'claim' the date, so there

won't be a similar event scheduled by another amateur theatre.

2. *Auditions*. If you're holding open auditions, do another press release. Try for coverage of the audition itself by a feature writer, TV crew, or radio news reporter. Call the editors and suggest an angle – such as the total reliance on local talent, or the mixture of old and young people at the auditions. You could also write a short feature story on audition anxiety or opportunities for aspiring actors and musicians. Be sure to notify all listings editors, in any case.

3. *Use press releases* to announce the audition results. Who was chosen for each major role? Why? What are their qualifications, backgrounds, other interests? The more local the paper or broadcast station, the more important names will be – so list everyone who's involved.

    Writers love anecdotes, so include short interesting or humorous ones that relate to the story. Did a young clarinet player do better at the auditions than more experienced musicians, and thus land her first paying job? Did the drummer forget his sticks and have to audition using kitchen knives? If so, include these items in your release or story.

4. *Feature it*. Write a feature story on the composer and/or playwright. Strive, as usual, for a tie-in with a relevant hook or news peg. Maybe the theme of the musical offers insights into modern life. Maybe its historical perspective presents a critical look at progress. Perhaps you can find a unique local connection.

    As the performance date nears, try for a feature story on the set design and construction or other production highlights. Again, look for a current trend that will broaden your appeal. For instance, is the set designer physically handicapped? Then slant your story that way. Has smoking been banned at rehearsals? Does the entire cast do 15 minutes of warm-up aerobic exercises before the rehearsal? Are the lights controlled by a computer? Find a tie-in that will interest people who don't care about the theatre. Then you've hooked a new audience.

5. *Up-to-the-minute promotion*. As the performance dates get closer, shift into high gear and double-check with media people to remind them – and urge them – to cover the big event. Be *sure* all events calendars have the information they need. Try for a slot on all the local news shows, and try to place a cast member or two on some chat shows. Other publicity ideas could be used now, too – posters on telegraph poles, flyers on community noticeboards, banners across the street near the theatre, a telephone ticket-sales contest.

6. *Reviews*. Send all reviewers in the area a packet of information that includes previous stories and releases. Be sure they have good seats for the dress rehearsal or first performance, and double-check with them by phone to be sure they've received the tickets, and to urge them to attend. (Don't, however, ask for a good review – the performance must stand on its own merits. Your job is just to be sure the reviewer attends.)

7. *Follow-up promotion*. After the performance, do a wrap-up article. How many hours went into the production? Any injuries? Any adversity overcome? Did the flautist's wife deliver a baby the night of the first performance? Did the

standing-room-only crowds buoy up the spirits of the producers? Are any cast members turning professional because of their experiences and reception in this performance?

If there is any special social, cultural or community angle involved, be sure to publicise that, too. Did the composer come down from London for the première? Was enough money raised to make the down-payment on a permanent home for the company? Or was the money raised given to a local charity?

Planning publicity this way is a lot of work, and in a project this big you should have a committee to help you. The hard work will pay off, though, when you meet all your goals and see a full audience applauding every performance.

In this example, the amateur theatre and orchestra represent a broad segment of people, and are therefore likely to be covered by the media in your area. However, if you are just one musician, or a for-profit band trying to get noticed, you'd follow the same steps. You'd try for strong tie-ins with trends, fads or newsworthy events to magnify your importance and relate your activities to popular causes.

If you're a pop band, for example, you wouldn't use most of the steps discussed above, but you'd formulate your own plan of action. You could:

● Plan your publicity campaign, map out your goals, and divide responsibility among the group's members.
● Issue a press release to announce opening night, or contract renewal, at the club where you work.
● Devise promotional activities, probably including the club owner, that would include the kind of hooks that would interest the media. Then you'd publicise these activities with press releases, calendar listings and feature stories. See Chapter Nineteen for ideas of events to publicise.
● Take advantage of the publicity angle of normal changes and events, when possible. If your drummer is leaving the band, why not hold auditions to find a replacement and publicise the auditions – even make it a contest? (You'll hire the replacement you want, of course, but why not make an event out of it?)

Publicity Practice

If you do this activity, it won't really be 'practice' – it will give you some much-needed information, and will save you time when you're actually publicising an event.

Look through your cuttings file, and newspapers and magazines, to find all the local *calendars of events* that you can. Don't overlook tabloids, weeklies, and free *shoppers newspapers*. Also, keep a list of which broadcast stations run *community calendars* that would be relevant to your musical activities.

Then call all the stations and papers. Ask to speak to the editor responsible for listings. Find out when their deadlines are, and how to submit items – on a three-by-five card, in a letter, by phone?

While you're on the phone, find out the same deadline information, and editors' names, for feature articles. Make a chart showing these deadlines. Call it the *contacts/deadline* chart, and include addresses, phone numbers and names for easy reference. Now you're ready to get listed when you have a concert, show, festival or anything else that should be publicised.

In even a medium-sized city, there is so much going on that the weekend listings are filled with events. The calendar editors aren't going to go looking out for you to find out what you're doing. You've got to tell them. And you'll have to tell them over and over again. Making the deadline chart will make getting listed easy for you.

It Works Both Ways

Once you've learned to prepare a *press release*, and you know more about the structure of newspapers and broadcast stations, you can jump right in and publicise yourself until you're rich and famous. Remember that *the media need you as much as you need them*.

Your job is to make your ideas interesting, to make them pass the 'so what?' test. You have to look outside yourself and your own needs to see how your music would appeal to others. Maybe you'll have to start some new projects that would help your publicity efforts.

The job of the media is to inform and entertain their readers, listeners and viewers. If you can help editors, writers, photographers and camera-men by letting them know how interesting your music and performances are, you've really done them a big favour – but they won't know about it unless someone – *probably you* – tells them.

CHAPTER ELEVEN

THE PRESS RELEASE

You're planning the publicity for your band's opening at a new club in town, and you've come up with a great idea – a *hook* – that would snare any editor's attention. What do you do now? Do you just call him on the phone? Should you write a letter? How, specifically, do you get the media interested in you and your projects?

You send a *press release*. It's a standard tool that works better than letters and phone calls; it's universally used to publicise people and events. The release is essentially a pared-down news story that presents the outline of your event in a way that will grab an editor's attention.

Why are press releases so popular? Because they tell your story at a glance. An editor can run the release exactly as you wrote it, call you for more details, or send a writer and photographer to cover your event. A good press release is part of virtually every publicity campaign, and yours should be no exception.

You'll send releases to all kinds of people besides those in the media, too. They're an ideal way to reach agents, club owners, your regular clients and even other musicians. Releases look professional, get attention, tell your story, impress your readers, and get you noticed.

The best part: producing a press release isn't difficult.

What events in your musical life need a press release? After all, you don't want to waste time publicising the wrong activities.

Anything that's newsworthy should be publicised, and you should define *newsworthy* as creatively as possible. Use your brainstorming lists from previous chapters and study your cuttings file. Scholarship awards, opening night for your band, formation of a new band, signing a record contract, production of a video, open auditions, and dates for concerts, shows and recitals are newsworthy, and a press release will help you spread the word.

Often, you won't really be trying for *news* coverage – you'll send a release to stimulate interest for a *feature* article – but you'll still use that hook or slant to relate your activities to something else.

A press release will help your musical activity get noticed by the media if:

1. *It's a first.* The first night of your engagement at Coconut Grove, the first all-girl rock band in the history of Lincolnshire, the first performance you've given since graduating from college, the first time bagpipes have been used in a fusion band – these happenings will benefit from well-written releases.

2. *It's a specific event* that will attract an audience. Concerts, recitals, plays, musicals, workshops, seminars, even speeches can be effectively publicised with press releases. Is your jazz group playing a be-bop concert to

commemorate Charlie Parker's birthday? Is your rock band opening for a well-known act?

3. *It's the oldest, newest, largest, most unusual.* If you regularly play a guitar that was made in 1879, if your high-school band is experimenting with prototype drums made of graphite, if your barbershop quartet uses wireless microphones, if your pop band is trying for a *Guinness Book of Records* endurance test – send a release.

4. *It involves a celebrity or noted expert.* If Terry Wogan visits your school to adjudicate a talent contest, if Dudley Moore will be featured pianist with your cabaret band, if Pete Townshend sits in with your group for a charity event, if Barbra Streisand records a song you wrote – send a press release.

In short, if your music is involved with anything that's likely to be interesting to a broad audience, use a release to publicise it. It may even be an event that's contrived solely for its publicity value, such as the *Guinness Book of Records* stunt, or a legitimate news story. In either case, the release is the proper way to tell the editor about it.

News doesn't always just happen. *Much* – some say *most* – of what you read in the papers and see on TV is planned news, carefully orchestrated to publicise someone or some event. You should do the same.

The ideas given above are typical of those that can be profitably publicised. Chapter Nineteen summarises these and adds more events that can be turned to good publicity for all kinds of musicians. You'll continue to think of many more.

When you've become experienced at generating your own publicity, you'll produce press releases almost without effort. You'll think, "We're adding an amateur participation night at the club for the next two months to stimulate business.We should send a release to generate some feature articles. Let's see . . . what kind of hook would work best?" That's how a successful publicity seeker operates; everything can be turned to good publicity with the right approach. The release is your standard weapon.

Writing The Release

Press releases are like little news stories, and they follow the same *inverted pyramid* form. It's a simple, direct format that gives the most important details first and adds more information as the story goes on. The idea is to give the facts and arouse the readers' interest so they'll read on. The inverted pyramid looks like this:

First comes the summary lead.
Then come more details.
Then more details.
More details.
More.

If an editor chooses to print your release exactly as it's written, this form lets him cut the story to fit the available space without losing the most important facts.

And it gives the main idea of your story in the first paragraph. So, to write a release, simply list everything you want to say. Use the old *5 w's and an h* formula as a guide, and fill in the blanks.

What _____
Who _____
Where _____
When _____
Why _____
How _____

Once you have the facts together, organise them with the most important point first. Is this a *when*-oriented event, like a concert? If so, put that first. Or is the *who* more important – Phil Collins, say, visiting your music shop to promote a new line of drums?

In writing a press release you're trying for publicity, true, but you're also writing news. All editors recognise puffery and unsupported self-promotion – and they'll reject any blatant attempts to use their media this way. Stick to the facts, but present them as interestingly as possible.

The Lead Paragraph

The first sentence of your release must demand attention. Editors are busy and overworked. They're inundated daily with releases from every organisation from the League of Women Voters to the Hog Growers' Association. How can you make your release stand out in this crowd? By using the strongest hook you can think of – in the first sentence.

Several approaches work for the lead:

- *Question*. "When is the last time you heard authentic, acoustic bluegrass music in a relaxing outdoor setting?"
- *Who*. "World-famous bandleader Ron Mendola will conduct the West of England All-Star Jazz Ensemble at . . ."
- *What*. "Synthesisers, new keyboard instruments that turn anyone into an instant composer, will be demonstrated Saturday, July 4, at . . ."
- *Where*. "London's famous Marquee club will be the venue for the first major performance of local band 5 Go Mad . . ."
- *Why*. "Because of renewed interest in early Black American music, the Allen Stone Quartet will present an evening of authentic Spirituals and early Blues at . . ."
- *How*. " 'Proper warm-up exercises for pianists can help avoid cramps and muscle fatigue,' says Dr Sandra Underwood, well-known sports medicine specialist."

Make that first line interesting and you've won the editor's attention. He'll read on to get the rest of your story, and (we hope) decide to print it. But if that first line is boring – "Joe's Band is proud to announce the addition of more first-rate equipment that will, we're sure, make us an even better band" – the story will never pass the editor's 'so what?' filter.

Finish writing the release by giving more details, in *descending order of importance*. Squeeze the who, what, where, why and possibly how, into the first two sentences if possible, and use the supporting, or less important, data in the final two or three paragraphs.

Here are more press release guidelines:

1. *Be brief*. Busy editors won't read through pages to get your story. Try to keep it to one page; two at the most. Don't tell everything you know. If an editor is interested, she'll contact you for more information.
2. *Use short sentences*. Newspaper columns are only around two inches wide, and one typewritten line from your release equals two lines of print in the paper. Keep paragraphs short, too; limit them to two or three sentences each.
3. *Add supporting names toward the end of the release*. Local papers like to print names, so list committee members, band members, and family names when it's appropriate. Larger papers will often cut the story before the names; smaller ones will include them.
4. *Use quotations*. Strong, appropriate quotations add spice to a story. They break up the greyness of long paragraphs and add an expert's authority to your story.
5. *Be accurate*. Sending press releases requires you to be responsible. Be positive that times, addresses, names and other facts are correct. Have someone else double-check for you. Remember that Johnson sounds like Johnston, Johnstone, Jonson, Jonsen, Janson and even Jensen. Be sure, of course, that everything is spelled right, but pay special attention to names – because people will complain to the editor if they're wrongly identified. Don't risk your credibility by inattention to details.

Press releases usually follow a standard format. First, the release should be typed, not typeset. Always double-space, on one side of the page only. Leave wide margins all around.

You can use a modified form of your letterhead for issuing press releases – but you'll need to add the words *Press Release* to show that this isn't just another letter.

Once you have the artwork, use the layout and paste-up techniques from Chapter Six to produce an interesting press release form. Then have your printer make as many copies as you'll need. When you're ready to send a release, follow the instructions below, typing in the headline and copy. You can have them duplicated for mailing by the printer, or just get them photocopied. (Whenever you send photocopies, of course, be sure that they're top quality, with crisp, black type, and no extraneous black specs or grey smudges.)

Flush against the right margin, type FOR IMMEDIATE RELEASE, or FOR RELEASE ON JULY 4,1999 if the story is date-specific.

Flush left, type FOR MORE INFORMATION, CONTACT: and give the name and phone number of whoever is available to talk to editors and reporters. Always include a contact name, even if the release is printed on your letterhead.

Use a headline, which can be flush left or centred, and should be all capital letters – DERBY BAND IS FINALIST IN NATIONAL 'STARS OF TOMORROW'

CONTEST. (Don't use a full stop in a headline, though.)

You may choose to run a short 'teaser' headline above the main one to attract further attention. "Local rock group is among 'best of the best'."

If the release is more than one page, type 'more' centred at the bottom of the first page, and put a short identifying headline, and the contact person's name and number on the second sheet. The second sheet should be a plain, non-letterhead page.

At the end of the release, type four # signs centred at the bottom of the page to indicate that there's no more.

PRESS RELEASE

FOR IMMEDIATE RELEASE

For more information, contact:
George Carere: (01) 234 5678

Local rock group is among 'best of the best'

DERBY BAND IS FINALIST IN NATIONAL 'STARS OF TOMORROW' CONTEST

Sheer Energy, a four-piece Derby rock band, has been named a finalist in the BBC's 'Stars of Tomorrow' national talent search. The four finalists, best of over two thousand initial entrants, will compete for a record contract and a £10,000 prize on a two-hour live TV special next autumn. The exact date will be announced by the BBC.

Band members George Dee, Mick Watts, Bill Martin and Doug Fairburn, all from Derby, are elated. "This may be the break we've been working for," says drummer Dee. "We tried other routes to get a record and we're really excited about this chance."

The hard-driving band specialises in a blend of thoughtful lyrics with Top-40 energy, but it shuns the high-tech approach that is popular in music today. "No computers, no synthesisers, no drum machines for us. We like the sound of guitars," says Watts, who plays lead guitar.

In the 'Stars of Tomorrow' contest, Sheer Energy competed against bands from all over the country to reach the final four. They are rehearsing new material that, they hope, will power them to a first-place finish.

"We want all our friends in Derby to be watching that show and cheering us on," adds Martin, the group's bassist and lead singer. "If we win, we'll throw a party that Derby will remember for years."

Sheer Energy was formed when all four musicians were studying electrical engineering at the University of Hull. They've been together for almost thirteen years, and have no plans to leave the music business.

# # # #

Smaller, local newspapers might print this release exactly as it's written, or they might trim it to fit their available space. Larger daily papers, and TV and radio stations, however, may choose to do their own stories, using their own writers and photographers.

This release should be sent as soon as the contest's finalists are announced, and should go to all papers in the area, including any university publications, to all relevant radio stations, and to the local TV stations. If Sheer Energy is really interested in maximum publicity, another release would announce the date of the TV special, and yet another release would cover the results. (Of course, if they won the contest, the TV network and the record company would send out their own press releases.)

The news tag here, obviously, is the band's excellent showing in a national contest – its chance at fame and, possibly, fortune. Even if Sheer Energy doesn't win the ultimate contest, it will reap loads of publicity from such efforts as this release, and its name will become synonymous with successful music.

You, too, should get in the habit of using press releases. It isn't difficult, it's the accepted form of reaching media outlets, it looks professional, and it's a very accepted way of blowing your own horn. After all, if you're doing something exciting and worthwhile, shouldn't you share it with the public?

Of course you should. And mark it 'For Immediate Release.'

CHAPTER TWELVE

GETTING NOTICED IN PRINT – NEWSPAPERS AND MAGAZINES

You have press releases in hand and you're planning a terrific music project that will, you're sure, interest everybody in town. You want newspaper stories – and perhaps a magazine feature. How do you proceed?

You find out what the media want, and what they're now using, and you shape your ideas to fit these guidelines. If you can give them the kinds of stories they need, you'll get lots of coverage. They'll call it 'news' or 'features'; you'll call it 'publicity.'

Newspapers exist to provide news, information and entertainment – but they couldn't survive without selling advertising, and commercial radio and TV stations also exist through advertising revenue. Always remember that the space devoted to your story represents lots of advertising income – space is expensive. A feature article on your band could easily take up the same space as a £500 ad – or a £5,000 one in a major newspaper. An interview with you on a talk show would be 'worth' lots of money if it were sold as ad time.

Since your media exposure is worth so much money, it will pay back the effort it takes. Remind yourself, as you're addressing your press releases, that the free publicity you get might be worth thousands of pounds.

On the other hand, no editors will give you free advertising. If they think that's what you're after they'll refer you to an ad salesman. You're trying for free publicity, sure, but it must involve a truly interesting event or personality.

This is such an important point that it should be repeated: *to get publicity from the media, your story ideas must be interesting in themselves.* Don't make editors or writers think you're trying to use them; work to make your story interesting for their readers.

This chapter discusses getting noticed in all kinds of newspapers, newsletters and magazines. Large daily papers, with circulations of hundreds of thousands, will help your career – and so will newsletters that cover just one neighbourhood.

Newspapers

Maybe you get your daily news from *The Times*, but you'll probably get the most publicity from smaller local papers. You might even do best, especially at first, with weeklies, or low-circulation speciality papers. Generally, the more local the paper, the better your chances for lots of publicity, because smaller papers concentrate on local events and personalities.

"But," you say, "newspapers seem so formal and complicated. Is it really possible to get them to notice my band?"

Yes. No newspaper can cover everything with its own staff or think of every interesting idea for a story. They do what they can, of course, with their staff people, but all editors welcome ideas – no matter what the source. They may not *use* every concept that's suggested, but if it's a good one they'll at least consider it.

So it's true. If you have good ideas for stories, newspapers need you.

What's useful to you in the paper? Lots. You'll find potential publicity in every section if you use the right hooks. You can be noticed with extensive coverage, photos, or simply the frequent mention of your name, in news stories, feature articles, reviews of performances or recordings, arts/music stories, business reports, editorials, letters to the editor, regular columns, and calendar-of-events listings.

There are two basic approaches to getting in the paper. You can write a letter to the editor (about raising the drinking age in your town, for example), or you can interest an editor enough to send a writer and photographer to cover the story. You can even write your own feature articles and submit them for publication – often with surprisingly good results.

How to Get in Touch

The organisational chart of a newspaper shows the publisher at the top, editors in the middle, and reporters and photographers at the bottom. Don't approach the publisher or the writers; go straight to an editor with your ideas.

The working, everyday decisions on what to cover are made by the *editors* – men and women who manage one interest-area of the paper. Larger papers have many editors – one for each section – and it's important to approach the right one with your ideas.

It's useful to think of editors as your primary audience; if your ideas don't interest them, the story won't get printed. Think of them as *screens*, or *filters* – they're looking for good ideas and discarding the boring, irrelevant, or self-serving ones.

Editors select what to cover and sometimes rewrite articles for publication. At smaller papers they often write stories as well, so remember that editors are always very busy. They'll rarely have time to chat on the phone about your ideas.

Since editors are generally overworked, make your contact with them business-like and brief – where appropriate, use the standard press release, not a five-page, rambling letter. Also, editors are always under deadline pressure, so try not to call at their busiest times; for morning papers, this is the preceding evening; for afternoon papers, the mornings are most rushed.

Before you call any editor, call the paper and ask for that editor's name. Do your best to stay current and keep up with job changes; editors, like everyone else, want to be addressed properly (with their names spelled correctly).

The easiest and most direct route to the proper editor is simply to call her (or her secretary), succinctly describe the story idea you have, and ask if she's the right person to get your press release. If not, she'll tell you who is. *Always send your press releases to a specific editor, never just to the newspaper*.

Which editor should you approach? News stories go to the *news editor*. Send him press releases about awards, fund-raising, college activities, major concerts, new buildings, and so on. Feature stories about your music and lifestyle issues or trends go to the *features editor*. Sometimes this department includes the society pages, which can be useful for stories pertaining to country clubs and activities of the well-to-do. And business, education, religion and sports stories have their own editors on mid-sized and larger papers. Direct specific ideas to the proper editor.

Reviews are important to every performer, and your paper will either have staff reviewers or use freelancers. Be sure the appropriate reviewer knows of upcoming concerts and appearances, gets plenty of advance information, and has good (complimentary, of course) seats.

Don't assume that the reviewer will be musically educated. You may have to subtly plant ideas and even provide clever phrases that aptly describe your music. If you have previous (good) reviews, include them in your press kit.

If you know when your performance will be reviewed, try to meet the reviewer. (Sometimes this isn't possible, of course, and some reviewers jealously guard their objectivity.) If you can, spend time talking with the reviewer to answer questions, give your own ideas, and to be sure that the reviewer knows what you're trying to do. If your band specialises in original material, be sure the reviewer knows it; and if you do only covers, tell her that too.

What if you receive a negative review? Unless it's totally, blatantly unfair, don't respond. You'll rarely win a battle with the media, so don't complain unless you're the unlucky recipient of a vicious hatchet job – which will probably never happen. If, though, your rock band is reviewed by someone who knows nothing about rock and roll – and hates it, besides – a polite letter of complaint, with copies to the editor, would be appropriate.

Reviewers are usually responsible people who enjoy the music they write about. They'll interview you and give their opinions to their readers. You should help them do a good job by providing lots of excellent background information about yourself, your band and your music. That's what your press kit is for – so be sure writers and reviewers get a complete packet of all the information you've prepared. Don't hold back; include photocopies of other articles and reviews that will impress the writer, validate your own importance, and perhaps even suggest a few phrases and ideas.

Columns appear regularly, and often deal with the 'Who's News' or 'Who's Doing What Around Town' kind of material. What you're after here is lots of mention of your – or your group's – name. Many columnists use answering machines to take items for their daily output, so it's a simple matter to provide a constant stream of jokes, anecdotes, funny or odd events you've seen (all musicians should have lots of terrific stories), and so on – even if it's unrelated directly to your music. You want your name mentioned, that's all.

In a gossip column, you'd be happy with an item such as this: "Slick Rick Bell, who mans the piano at Snoot's Brasserie, was surprised last Tuesday when local MP George Jones stopped in for a visit. Slick Rick reports that Jones's voice is in great shape – and sounds ready for next month's bi-election campaign."

The Calendar of Events may take up several pages in the *Saturday Leisure Guide,* or it may be just a few lines in a smaller paper. In any case, all your musical activities that qualify should be listed. Call the Calendar editor (or whatever he is known as – titles may vary from paper to paper) for deadline information; send your release, or a short statement of what's happening, to that editor. It wouldn't hurt to follow up with a phone call to be sure the release was received.

The calendar editor may not want to list your appearance at a night-club, since it's not a non-profit event. After all, the calendar isn't an advertising vehicle for private businesses. So you may have to use your publicity ingenuity to create a musical happening worthy of mention. (See Chapter Nineteen and use your imagination.)

For example, if you're in a pop band, don't just go to work at the club every week, playing for the same old half-empty room. Instead, think of a special promotion, a celebration you could sponsor, and get it publicised in every calendar of events in town. Hold a celebration of the Midsummer Solstice, or an American-style Thirties theme party on the day Prohibition was repealed, or an 'Aerobics on the Dancefloor' contest. Find an interesting hook and publicise it.

Thus, the calendar of events editor might ignore a notice that simply states, "Joe's Band plays nightly at The Blue Note Club," because that looks like free advertising. However, if your notice reads: "Joe's Band welcomes would-be musicians for guest performances every Tuesday night, and holds old-fashioned jam sessions on Wednesdays at the Blue Note Club" you'd have a better chance, because jam sessions and open microphones appeal to the public.

Does the calendar editor ever print pictures to go with listings? If yours does, be sure to send a photo along.

Cover It

When you send your release to the paper, include a simple covering letter, addressed to the editor you want to reach. Such a covering letter *must be short* – its only task is to introduce the release. Tell, as briefly as possible, what the release says, and why it's important and interesting. If you can think of a short illustration that supports the release, include it.

Don't ask, beg, or cajole the editor to cover your story. Just make your letter and release so interesting that they demand attention.

Working with Reporters

When an editor likes your ideas enough to send a reporter and perhaps a photographer, you'd better be on time for your appointment. Remind your band that you're scheduled to meet a photographer at ten o'clock tomorrow morning, and give the drummer a wake-up call if he tends to oversleep. Reporters and photographers are very busy, and won't wait for you – or your sleepy drummer.

During the interview, work to establish a good rapport with the writer. If you're at home, offer him a cup of coffee; be relaxed, friendly, and natural. Don't try to impress him, and don't argue with him – just do what you can to help him write an interesting story about your music.

Never tell a reporter what to include. That's his job, and he's proud of his abilities and independence. Answer his questions, and volunteer information, but don't try to dictate the form or content of the article.

Remember that there's nothing wrong with saying "I don't know" when you don't. Evasive or defensive answers can work against you more than an admission of ignorance. "No, I really can't remember when Oscar Peterson made his first record," is a much better answer than, "Nobody cares about that old acoustic jazz any more." The first is simply an honest answer, while the second makes the respondent look narrow-minded and uneducated. And perhaps the reporter is a jazz buff whose favourite pianist is Oscar Peterson.

Similarly, never say anything negative about other performers. Sure, music usually isn't controversial, but reporters always look for something spicy to enliven their stories; if you don't want to be quoted on something, the safest course is not to say it; with many reporters, nothing is ever really 'off the record.'

Don't ask to see, or check over, an article after it's written. Sometimes a writer will ask you to read a piece for accuracy, but usually reporters won't allow anyone except editors to alter their work. Just provide your best facts, anecdotes, ideas and angles, and let them put the story together.

Don't ask the reporter when the story will be printed. That's the editor's decision, and reporters usually can't predict which of their stories will run, or when.

Send a short thank-you note to the reporter and/or editor after your story runs. Don't thank them for running the story, because that's their job, after all, but let them know you appreciate the excellent work they did. If you didn't like the way something was presented, don't complain unless it was a major error; nit-picking will make the editor think you're a pest, and your access to that paper will disappear.

Keep sending a steady stream of ideas, news releases, column tid-bits, and even fully written stories to your paper. To some extent, getting noticed in newspapers is a numbers game – the more you submit, the more mention you get. Don't expect every one of your ideas to be printed, but don't give up. Remember: newspapers must have articles and your ideas are important. Keep them coming.

Different Kinds of Papers
Your publicity needs as many outlets as you can find, so try to get noticed in all the papers in your area. They aren't all the same, however; each has its special niche in the news community, and will be able to help you in a different way, with different readers.

Large daily newspapers are the hardest nut to crack in your search for publicity because they cover the biggest area and must appeal to the broadest range of readers. Further, you'll encounter more competition from other publicity seekers. Don't let this stop you from trying, but realise that your carefully worded press release may be one of a hundred that an editor receives each day.

Smaller, suburban dailies are a better bet. Large metropolitan areas often have several small papers, each serving a specific area. Make these a major target.

Weeklies offer excellent publicity possibilities because they often ignore 'hard news' and concentrate entirely on feature stories. At smaller papers, try to establish a personal relationship with the editor – deliver your press release in person (but don't stop to chit-chat – these editors are busy, too). Arrange to visit on the day *after* the paper comes out, never the day before – call ahead to find out when deadline pressure is at its worst.

The smaller the paper, the more local news is printed, and many small-town newspapers rely heavily on college, community and arts events. Here's where your press release will often be printed verbatim, and where the stories you write will find the warmest reception. Names are more important, too, to smaller papers, and group photographs have a better chance of being printed here. Emphasise items of community interest and push the neighbourhood angles – small papers usually focus on what's close, and of local, immediate interest.

Special interest publications are terrific publicity outlets for musicians and performers. If you can tie your music to a news or feature story that appeals to these specialised audiences – weekly sing-along evenings for retired citizens, for example – you'll find that these papers provide an excellent path to good publicity.

College papers are a valuable training-ground for journalists and serve college communities. Even if you aren't involved with a local college, keep it informed of musical activities that relate to college students – this is particularly important for contemporary music groups that play to student audiences. Young people are often more interested than the general public in new developments in music, and may be very receptive to what you're doing.

If you now attend, or graduated from, an institution in your area, you have a special reason to have your activities noticed there.

Free papers are primarily advertising vehicles, but many of them print feature articles and events calendars to attract readers. Collect these publications, and put them on your publicity list.

All these newspapers need articles, and if you simply slant your story idea to their particular audience, your publicity offerings will be well received.

Don't forget to save all the cuttings that mention you and your music. Sure, you want to tell the public what you do, but you want to keep proving to yourself that your publicity efforts are paying off. Your personal cuttings file will keep pace with your growing career, and each piece can be added to your press kit, or quoted in future brochures.

Newsletters

Newsletters are specialised publications for people who are interested in specific subject areas – neighbourhood developments, news of interest to banjo players, or information for collectors of old Cola bottles, for example. They are usually printed on standard-sized typing paper, and often have only four to eight pages. They may be distributed free, or sold by subscription.

Newsletters provide up-to-date information for club members, company employees, hobbyists, and any other group of people you can imagine. You can use such newsletters to get noticed.

Start by getting your musical activities mentioned in local newsletters that serve education, business, religious, neighbourhood, or other interests. Think of these newsletters as little newspapers, aimed at a very select audience.

Ask your clients about publicising your music through their newsletters. Companies, large hotels, resorts and even restaurant chains produce newsletters for their employees. When you perform for these clients, be sure that you're mentioned, reviewed, publicised and touted. If you have to write the copy yourself – do it, and slant it toward the newsletter's audience. Say what your music will do for *them*, and why they'll enjoy your band.

Neighbourhood associations publish newsletters, many active churches use them, and estate agents sometimes print their own newsletters for past and future clients. When you're playing for a community fund-raiser, college event, church party or street dance, get it mentioned. What you're after, of course, is constant notice, so that your name-recognition grows and stays high.

Don't scoff at a neighbourhood newsletter that only goes to 300 homes; there may be 20 prospective brides, two convention planners, and one booking agent who live in the neighbourhood, all of whom might need your services for their own events. You never know when publicity will pay off.

Many newsletters are published essentially by one person, who does everything from writing to mailing. Often such publisher/editor/writers are desperate for current news items about their subject areas, so help by sending your pertinent news releases. If you can give a newsletter an exclusive *scoop*, the editor will appreciate it and remember you next time you have a project to publicise.

When you find a publication that might be useful in your publicity efforts, save it. You'll be amazed at how many newsletters you'll discover in your own community, so always be on the alert for new ones. Keep samples, even if you don't have an immediate use for them – sooner or later, your publicity ideas will include them all.

Publicity Practice

It's time for another list. But this one doesn't require brainstorming; this one depends on research.

As you develop contacts with newspapers, newsletters and broadcast people, keep a *media-contacts* list. When you reach an editor, work with a writer on a story, or locate a chat-show host who loves your kind of jazz, enter the names, phone numbers and addresses on your list.

Keep a file card for each contact, and jot down comments that will further your relationship with that person. If an editor not only runs your story but tells you that he's an amateur trombonist – write it down. There may be an occasion when you can combine your need for publicity with that editor's desire to play his trombone.

Your *media-contacts* list should be separate from the target audience list you started in Chapter Two. The media people should get a steady stream of information about your activities, while prospective employers should, in addition, get your sales pitch.

Magazines

Two kinds of magazines will help you publicise your musical activities. The first is the *general interest* magazine. Such magazines focus on people and events of interest to the general public. Since monthly magazines have a long preparation time and early deadlines (often three months – or more – before the publication date), they rely on interesting feature stories rather than news.

If your story involves a continuing event, an annual celebration, or profiles of interesting community people, these magazines provide an excellent outlet; but they won't usually use timely information or news-related, one-time stories. Read a few issues to get a feel for the kinds of features these magazines like.

You should also take advantage of magazines written for and by musicians. Whatever your musical speciality, there's a magazine for it – whether you're a drummer, keyboardist, church choir director, electronic music experimenter, or brass band conductor. You'll benefit, of course, by reading these magazines to stay up to date, but you should also strive to enhance your image by being the *subject* of in-depth articles in such publications.

The Main Feature

Full-length feature articles should be among your primary publicity goals. Work towards having them written *about you and your musical activities*. Or, if you can, write them yourself.

Keep a magazine's audience in mind when you approach an editor or send a press release. Magazines are almost always targeted to a specific group, and your story should offer insight, entertainment or useful information. Magazine features are often longer and more in-depth than newspaper articles, so they must be informative and interesting to keep readers involved.

Why not try to interest the editor of a business magazine in an article called "How Music Can Motivate Your Sales Staff"? You could write it, or work with a staff reporter.

Maybe you're part of the 'below-the-line' recording industry – often heard in jingles, but not known by the public. Suggest a feature on studio musicians – "Britain's 'Sixty Second' Men (and Women)." If your rock band has been around for 15 years, you probably have enough interesting stories and anecdotes for a book, but send a few of your best tales (the clean ones) to whet an editor's appetite for a piece called "The View from the Stage – Joe's Band Tells All."

When you, your band or your event gets a feature article in a magazine, it means that you're well on your way to a successful performance career. But don't stop – start thinking about your next interesting activity for the next article.

Here are a few more ideas for getting good magazine publicity:

Write a letter to the editor about a controversial issue, to add information to a recent article, or just to praise the magazine for its content and style. If you think

Harmonica Happenings, for example, did a terrific job covering the annual harmonica enthusiasts convention, write a letter of commendation. Just having your name in print will make your name stand out among harmonica players.

Keep it short. Most magazines use *fillers* – short news items or anecdotes that fill blank space at the end of articles. Jokes, hints or anecdotes are good fillers, and you'll usually receive credit – and sometimes money – for each one that's used. For instance, did your pop band play Christmas parties for every major bank in town? If you can come up with a humorous angle, write a couple of paragraphs about it – "Bank Parties Get High Interest from Joe's Band."

More and more magazines run several pages of short *featurettes* – 100- to 300-word pieces on an interesting person or event. Match your angle to the magazine's overall slant and regularly submit such one-page items – about you and your music, of course. Thus, do a short piece for a lifestyle magazine on "The Ten Most Unusual Places in Town to Hold a Party." Or send a short to one of the drum magazines on "The Drummer's Emergency Tool Kit." Get your name in print, save those cuttings, and you're on your way to becoming an unrecognised expert in the field.

Tourists count, too. A useful sub-category of magazines is the tourist guides you'll see in hotels and at tourist destinations. They always include a 'Nightbeat' or 'What's Happening After Dark' column (often limited to clubs that buy advertising in the magazine, however). If you play in a club, urge your employer to advertise, and then push for a feature article on your group – or at least listing in the events calendar. This is particularly important if you play a less popular kind of music – jazz, for example – because those out-of-towners looking for jazz will never find you otherwise.

Convention and tourist money is important to the economics of many cities – and many musicians. Travellers often spend more time and money on entertainment when they're on vacation – so be sure they know where to find your music.

Such magazines are usually found only in hotel lobbies or rooms, or at Tourist Information Centres. Add them to your media list if they match your needs.

What? Me a Writer?

Why not write articles on your music and submit them to appropriate magazines? You're already preparing your own press releases, so why not do longer pieces as well?

Professional journals often don't demand perfect writing. The editors know that you're a musician first, and they're more interested in the information you can share with their readers than your writing style. They'll fix your punctuation errors. So if you've discovered a new way to programme your synthesiser, why not share it with other keyboard players?

Most magazines will send a free *house style* sheet that tells how to submit articles and photographs for publication.

Most, but not all, magazines pay for articles they publish. Even when rates aren't high, it's nice to be paid for your ideas. So, if you have a unique approach to finding new students for your teaching studio, why not write about it? You'll help the readers, and yourself.

As a writer, your status as an expert will grow. If you write an article on "Caring for Your Piano" for *Music Teacher*, reprints of that article will add clout to your publicity kit because they'll impress potential clients with your expertise. An article in *Wire* magazine on "Northern Jazz – The Laid-Back New Wave" with your by-line will enhance your standing among other musicians as well as editors and the public.

If you're interested in writing for magazines, go ahead and try. Since you're an expert by now at identifying hooks and relating music to trends and news issues, you'll be a natural. Hooks and trends are exactly what magazines want.

Again, save everything that's printed about you. Send photocopies of relevant articles along with your promotional material, because each article about – or by – you will validate your status, make it obvious that you're important, and will underscore your professional ability.

Help those editors fill their pages, and they'll help you fill your calendar with productive dates.

CHAPTER THIRTEEN

YOU'RE ON THE AIR

Almost everybody listens to the radio and watches television, and that makes these media prime publicity outlets for you. Lots of people don't read newspapers, many don't subscribe to magazines – but most of them watch the Six o'Clock News and listen to the radio while they drive. Shouldn't they hear about your music?

If you can get on the air, you'll have a large audience. The Six o'Clock News will make you famous – for a short time. Stories can be covered live, and broadcast deadlines are measured in minutes, not days or weeks. And TV is dynamic – the addition of sight and sound adds impact to your story. It also conveys the image of success. For some reason, being on TV gives you a kind of celebrity status.

However, there's lots of competition for air-time. Many people try to build their entire publicity and advertising programmes around radio and TV, so programme directors and news editors have lots of requests for coverage.

And broadcasts offer only fleeting exposure. You may be forgotten as soon as you're off the air. People sometimes save newspaper articles, but when broadcasts are over they're usually gone for good.

How can you get noticed on radio and TV? Your activities can be covered on news or feature programmes. You can be interviewed on chat shows. You could even produce your own show. In this chapter we'll discuss exactly how to go about using these publicity outlets.

Different Stations For Different People

There is a wide variety of local and national radio and TV stations, both public service (BBC) and commercial (independent), so whatever your musical interests, there's a broadcast outlet to match them.

And don't forget *cable*. As it becomes increasingly available, television will change radically. No longer will the viewer be limited to just four channels – subscribers will get dozens of channels. Most of these cable outlets won't originate in your area, but some will, and you'll find television becoming a more accessible publicity medium today than it has been up till now. Diversity brings opportunity.

It's Happening Now

Sometimes immediate, or live coverage will be important – the grand opening of your town's restored concert hall as it happens, for example. A local station might do a remote broadcast of your 'Live Monday Night Jazz' from a local club. A TV personality could interview you on the air the day your record is released. And broadcast media can announce the cancellation of your concert because of snow – or the last minute addition of a second performance.

Aside from fast-breaking news, though, most radio and TV stories have special needs. To be interesting, broadcast events must be:

1. *Active.* What's active? A concert, a back-stage view of a musical theatre production, an instrumental workshop, an 'open' orchestral rehearsal – all would make interesting television.
2. *Current.* Last week's news and events are old stuff to broadcast media. If it's current they'll be interested; otherwise, no. Television producers are very aware of what's hot and what's not.
3. *Aurally or visually exciting.* You'll get the best coverage if your music sounds – and looks – exciting. If you can promise a TV producer that he'll get colourful shots of your amateur operatic society performing an intricately choreographed number, he may be interested; but if all you have to offer is a routine stage concert he probably won't cover it. Television depends on visual excitement.
4. *Simple.* Your story must be easy to tell in a minute or two, because in a news or feature segment that may be all you get. Newspapers can take half a page to tell your band's story, but a television station may give you two minutes and 15 seconds. In such events, try to emphasise the big issue, the most important points, but leave the details for the print media.

Getting Noticed on Radio and TV

What kind of publicity opportunities do radio and television offer? Lots. Both news and feature stories will appeal to TV producers and audiences, and the distinction between them isn't always clear. In fact, many TV news-people emphasise personality more than content, style more than substance. If your event is timely, has lots of human interest, includes a strong visual element, can be summed up succinctly, appeals to a broad range of people, and has an irresistible hook, it may be a natural for TV, regardless of whether it's called news or feature material.

Broadcast News

"News," the old cliché goes, is an abbreviation for "North, East, West and South." The idea is that the news covers what's happening, everywhere. Of course, it's not possible for reporters to cover everything, so choices must be made. Broadcast news is so limited by time and technical considerations that it has to be more selective – you'll have a better chance for coverage if you emphasise that your event is *timely, controversial or new.*

Timely events such as concerts, plays, recitals, fund-raising activities, community events and grand openings can all involve music, be promoted in advance, and be covered live. If your band is producing a local 'We Are the World'-type song to raise money for the homeless, try for live coverage of your introductory concert. It's news.

Controversy is a staple of news departments, so watch for it. If the musician's union is on strike and picketing, if the college music faculty is arguing whether to add a course in rock music history, if city police start arresting street musicians, if your rock band is fighting the local council for permission to hold an outdoor concert – it's news.

Changes are also news. Did a new music director take over at the only school in town? Has a landmark jazz club switched to a punk format? If these events would interest many people, they're news.

Features

Often, radio and TV features are an important part of evening newscasts. Local news shows rely heavily on *lifestyle* stories, and are excellent possibilities for your publicity. Regardless of whether your event is news- or feature-oriented, you should provide ideas – and a visual hook, if you're trying for TV – to grab an audience's attention.

Anything *unusual* offers an excellent peg for broadcast features. Do you collect antique instruments? A radio feature on you playing (or trying to play) the serpent or the cornetto could be the peg for a feature about your hobby. Is your band the first in your area to use only electronic instruments – including drums? Or does your band use only unamplified acoustic instruments? Since radio and television are sound-oriented, why not let the angle be your sound itself?

As with newspaper features, the *oldest, youngest, newest, most advanced* anything can be featured. Is your first school rock band – formed in 1955 – having a reunion concert now that you're all nearly 50 years old? And are your kids giving their first concert the same night? A 'battle of the rock generations' story would be a good TV feature.

Lifestyle stories are popular for broadcast media. Work with whatever trend is current at the moment to find an angle that will interest the producers. Is the female singer in your rock band pregnant? How about a lifestyle item called 'Local rock band's musical conception'? Is a local part-time big band, 'Doctors and Nurses', composed entirely of medics – who are sometimes called to the hospital in the middle of a dance job? It's a natural for a lifestyle feature. Does your pop band change styles one Sunday evening each month to perform old favourites at a retirement home?

When you're thinking about broadcast publicity, remember that on-location items are expensive to produce – especially for television. Where a newspaper would assign a reporter with a notebook and pencil, a television station must send a reporter, a camera operator, and a sound engineer – and that's just the beginning. Back at the station, editors, mixers and special effects people may work on the piece with £50,000 worth of electronic equipment. Don't be disappointed if a station doesn't rush out to cover every concert you do, but keep trying to make your events so interesting they can't be ignored.

Chat Shows

Would you like to talk for half an hour about your music on the radio, answering questions from callers – and promoting yourself all the while? That's the opportunity chat shows and phone-ins offer, and that's why they're one of the best publicity outlets anywhere. Authors, inventors, politicians and experts in many fields try to get chat show exposure, which can range from national network shows to small, local outlets.

To get booked on a chat show, do something interesting, controversial or new that would be a good subject for conversation with the public. If you've written a book or made a hit record you'll have little problem getting invited, but if you aren't yet well-known, you may have to be creative.

Think about what you have to offer – not what you can get. Remember, air-time is expensive, and no producer will put you on for an hour of free self-promotion. You've got to have something to give the listeners.

You can offer entertainment, information or help. You can tell listeners how to save money, attain self-fulfilment, or make themselves popular. You can be a visiting expert who answers trivial or important questions. Whatever you propose, however, must be interesting or important.

For instance, if you're an expert at piano tuning and repair, suggest a chat show spot on 'Buying and maintaining a piano.' Have you had a couple of songs published? That puts you ahead of most songwriters, and probably makes you a local expert. Try for a 'How to Get Your Songs Published' spot. Or maybe you know absolutely everything there is to know about The Beatles. How about a 'Stump the Expert' show, possibly timed to coincide with an important Beatles anniversary? Trivia contests are chat show standards. Use books of important and unusual anniversaries and celebrations to find a logical date to link with your idea. (More ideas for publicity hooks are provided in Chapter Nineteen.)

Listen carefully to the chat shows you'd like to be on. What kind of guests do they usually book? What's the focus? Is there an angle, a slant that matches your ideas? Would your interests correspond with those of the audience? If it's commercial radio, listen to the ads – they provide a clue to the make-up of that show's audience. Are the commercials aimed at people who would have no interest in your music – or at those who would share your concerns? You can learn a lot about a chat show by becoming a regular listener.

Every chat show or phone-in has a producer – the person who books the guests, screens the calls, and probably keeps the show coherent and running smoothly. Often the host mentions the producer's name on the air; if not, call the station and ask. If you have an idea that you think would appeal to her, send your publicity material along with a short covering letter detailing your proposal. Make it interesting and illustrate how it would appeal to the show's audience. Follow up with a phone call – *not* during the show's broadcast time – a week later.

If you have been on other shows, include a cassette of your appearance to prove that you're a good guest. If you haven't, send your press kit and emphasise your tie-in with a larger, important issue. Tell them about the work your band does with ghetto kids, or the money you've raised for urban renewal, or the free concert you played for the women's shelter. Make your proposal relevant. Tell them that you'll entertain the audience with tales of the early days of the big bands, or recent bits of rock trivia. Offer to demonstrate your ability, on the air, to make up calypso songs based on callers' suggestions. It has to be interesting, fun, up-beat, though. You probably won't find any chat show hosts that would like a guest to demonstrate all the members of the woodwind family.

To get ready for a broadcast appearance, practise with a tape recorder (or video camera if you're going to be on TV). Get friends to interview you, and ask difficult, even nasty, questions. Don't get flustered, mad or defensive. If a caller asks, "What makes you such a hot-shot expert anyway?" or, "If you know so much, why aren't you rich?" – what would you say? Practice will give you confidence.

Practice with a recorder will also highlight annoying verbal habits you may have. Do you say "you know" every other sentence? Do you rely on "uh," or have a nervous laugh? You can change these habits, and if you're trying for lots of broadcast publicity, you'll find it helpful to work on how you sound and look.

TV Appearances

So you're booked on the 'lifestyle' segment of the midday news to talk about your new computer-assisted music lessons for pre-school children. How do you behave, and what do you wear, to look polished and cool?

Several factors determine how you'll appear on TV. Your demeanour, the way you talk and answer questions, how relaxed you are, and even what you wear all work together to make you seem ill at ease – or to make you look like a video pro.

Clothes are important for television appearances, so think again about the image you want to project. You may have to plan an outfit that will look right on TV – and different broadcasts will have different needs.

If your band is being taped on location there's no problem – just wear what you always wear when you perform. But if you're being interviewed for a news or feature spot, or if you're a guest on *Pebble Mill At One,* you'll need to give some thought to what you wear. Jeans and flannel shirts, or metallic trousers, may not be right for lunchtime television.

For local interview or news items you should dress more conservatively than usual – especially if there's a question of what to wear. Sure, celebrities on *Wogan* can get away with looking dishevelled (with each hair carefully arranged to look carelessly tousled), but you aren't a celebrity, and local television has different expectations from prime-time network shows.

Practise with a video camera. Large cities have video-coaching firms that teach business executives how to be telegenic and believable on the air – but such professional coaching is expensive. You can get much the same valuable experience by using a home video camera to tape yourself in an interview or performance situation. If you don't have a video camera of your own, borrow one from a friend, or hire it from a video shop. All you need is the chance to see yourself on the screen.

The cardinal rule of video is don't look at the camera. Just keep your eyes on the host and ignore the camera. The exception is if you're making an appeal directly to the viewers, but this is rare.

Be sure your clothes fit, are fresh from the laundry with neat creases. If you must eat on the way to the studio be careful – that's the very time you'll spill soup on your tie or blouse. Polish your shoes, too, and wear over-the-calf socks. Also, TV cameras make you look a bit heavier than you are, so if you have a weight problem, wear dark colours and avoid patterns that would make you appear larger. Loose-fitting clothing is also more attractive than tight.

Ask the producer what colours photograph best, or watch the show in advance to see how the host dresses. Bright colours sometimes tend to 'bleed,' patterns distort, white glares, and black looks dead. If you can, wear earth tones and subtle colours. And avoid dark glasses (or photosensitive ones); they make you look sinister.

Men with heavy beards should shave just before the broadcast if possible. It may be helpful to use a smoothing pancake make-up to cover bags under your eyes (were you playing late last night?) and skin blemishes – but try them out before you get to the studio.

Your Own Show

Well, it's a long-shot, but why not try? If you're an expert in a particular kind of music, why not propose a radio show specialising in that format? If there is little or no independent programming for jazz, bluegrass, folk, ethnic, blues, electronic, new-age, Latin, classical, choral or chamber music in your area, this could be an enjoyable way to publicise your kind of music – and yourself as well.

If you're interested in producing such a show, call the station's programme director and explain your proposal. Volunteer to bring in a sample tape, or ask for an off-the-air audition.

Try an approach like this. "Hi, Mr. Programme Director. I'm Joe Jones, and I have a programme idea that I believe you would be interested in. I'd like to host a weekly jazz hour on your station. Jazz is gaining popularity, and has a devoted following – I've checked with several record shops, and they all report growing sales of jazz albums. Since no jazz at all is broadcast on independent radio in our area, I'm sure we could attract listeners, and I'm qualified to do the show – I have a degree in music education, and I earn my living as a jazz musician. My performance background has taught me to speak well. I understand mike techniques, and I've worked around electronics all my life. I'd even be able to programme the shows from my own record collection if the station's jazz resources are limited. I believe we could develop a new and loyal group of listeners for your station with just a little work."

This approach shows the programme director that you've done a bit of market research, and that you're aware of how important the audience size is to his station. You've shown that you're qualified, and that this venture wouldn't cost the station a lot of money.

There are plenty of pop and rock music experts already on the air. You'll have the best chances of success with other types – and you'll reap the best publicity if you match your broadcast efforts with the kind of music you perform.

More On-the-Air Ideas

Try to link your performances with someone else's broadcast when possible – and be sure that you're mentioned by name. If your dixieland band is attracting crowds at a charity event, and a local station is doing a remote broadcast, try to make sure that your band is featured several times during the afternoon. This way you *piggyback* your publicity onto the charity's.

And don't overlook the possibilities of educational programming. Even a locally produced show such as 'How to Play Folk Guitar,' or 'Reading Music for Beginners' would raise your recognition level, give you valuable experience, and probably pay you a fee. Many stations, of course, would rely on professional teachers for such broadcasts, but a creative approach, talent and enthusiasm might prevail. Who knows? Your idea might work so well that your show gets a regular spot – and creates a new career for you.

Also try to publicise your band's music on appropriate programmes. If you have a terrific tape of an original top-40-style tune, visit appropriate stations and try to get it aired. Even though many stations play only what's on the charts at the moment, some will play your work.

Some stations even run items featuring local musicians. If you've produced a record, you'll need to really pursue this avenue, with all the publicity tricks you can muster; but even if you only have a demo tape, work at getting it aired.

Remember, always get tapes of your broadcast appearances. Call in advance and ask the producer whether the station will make a copy for you (if you supply the blank cassette, of course). If so, find out what format they use. It's also a good idea to get a friend to record the broadcast at home, too, in case something goes wrong with the station's copy. Several performance tapes will be very useful in putting a good demo together.

Radio and TV broadcasts travel at the speed of light, and your appearances may seem to be forgotten just as quickly. Continue to establish good media contacts and develop ideas for coverage, though, because the net effect of all your appearances will be great publicity. One interview may not make you famous, but several can make you a local celebrity.

People will ask, "Didn't I see you on TV?" You'll smile and answer, "All the time." But don't tell them how you arranged all those appearances in the first place. Let them think that you're just a natural.

CHAPTER FOURTEEN

IT'S IN THE POST

Why should anyone go to the trouble to write a letter when it's so easy to pick up the telephone? After all, isn't this the age of instant communication?

True, telephoning is easy and quick – but letters remain an important publicity tool for your performance career. Well-written letters enhance your image – and they'll make your professional life run more smoothly than an unending series of phone calls. Business-people rely on letters of all kinds, and you should show your clients and prospective employers that you understand how things work in the business world. A clean, well-written letter of introduction shows that you care enough about that client's business to spend the time necessary to communicate clearly. Further, your personalised letterhead shows that you're established and serious about your image.

In fact, a well-done business letter, carefully typed on your handsome letterhead, puts you on equal footing with every other business or competitor, regardless of size or reputation. Your client needn't know that you borrowed the typewriter, or that your office is really the kitchen table. If your business correspondence looks good, you look good. In short, a well-done letter says a lot more about you than just the message it carries.

People will read your letters at their convenience, whereas they might not return your phone calls. Business-people value their time, and letters give them a way to control it, so letters are often more appreciated than phone calls. Letters don't interrupt important meetings. Phone calls are forgotten, misinterpreted or ignored – but letters are answered, filed, passed around for others to read, and kept for future reference. Letters last.

Letters also save money if you're dealing with an out-of-town client. Why make a series of long-distance calls when a letter will serve the same purpose – only better? Plus, it always helps to get it in writing. Specific details should be down in black and white to avoid errors. When people read and write letters and sign contracts they pay close attention. You'll avoid mistakes by using written confirmations. For example, a client may forget to tell the band about time or date changes. If you have a written, signed confirmation for Friday night, the client can't blame you for not showing up on Thursday. Letters help you protect yourself.

Mass mailings allow you to deliver a message inexpensively to your target audiences. You should build, and keep, mailing lists of those who need to know about your activities. Is such *direct-mail* publicity effective? Look in your post for the answer. If so many companies rely on it, you can be sure that it works for them – and mailings will work for you, too.

Do You Know All The Letters?

You'll depend on different kinds of letters in publicising your career, and while they're easy to write, they have different styles and purposes.

1. *Letters of introduction* will tell prospective clients about you and your music. Often, introductory letters prepare a client for your sales call so he'll already know who you are – and what you do. *Covering letters* that you send with press releases and other publicity information are like introductory letters – they 'introduce' the material you're sending, and reinforce the message.

2. *Other business letters* of all kinds are also important. You'll write to confirm details, to make proposals, to sell your music, to ask for information, or to request overdue payment. Letters have more impact than phone calls, and often get better results.

3. *Confirmations and contracts* aren't really letters – often you'll use standard forms and just fill in the blanks. They are written communication, however, so we'll discuss how you can best use them.

4. *Thank-you notes* are as important as anything else you do in your publicity programme. When you've played a job and taken the client's money (whether a little or a lot), *always* send a thank-you note. It's an extra step that every client will appreciate, remember and probably talk about. And saying 'thank you' is not just good business – it's also normal courtesy.

Believe it or not, a simple thank-you note can be one of the most effective aspects of your publicity programme. Don't just take the money and run. It's much better to take the money, say 'thank you,' and run.

Just My Type

Business letters usually follow a well-established pattern. You've probably picked this up somewhere along the line, but since you're not aware of the publicity value of everything you do, let's have a recap.

Appearance matters in business communication – and this means that your *business letters must be typed*. Hand-written business letters convey just one message: regardless of content, they say, 'amateur.' There aren't too many hard-and-fast rules concerning publicity, but this is one.

If you don't have a typewriter, why not buy one? Excellent machines cost much less today than they did just a few years ago. You can buy a sophisticated electronic typewriter for less than two hundred pounds. You don't type? It's not that hard – you can easily teach yourself or take an inexpensive course. An alternative, of course, is to arrange for someone else to do your typing, but this is cumbersome and can be expensive.

Keep your typewriter clean and well adjusted. Use black ribbon only – save the colours for writing to your fiancé. Use only typefaces that look like a typewriter – never use script or other fancy styles in business correspondence, because they may be hard to read, and they don't look business-like.

Use a computer, if you have one, but be sure it has a *letter quality printer*. Unless a dot-matrix printer really produces "near letter quality" results, don't use it to produce business correspondence – it's harder to read, because each letter is composed of tiny dots rather than solid lines.

If you do use a computer for correspondence, be sure that the right margin prints uneven, or *ragged right*, just as it would be if you'd typed the letter on a typewriter. Justified (that is, even) right margins look artificial and make letters look impersonal, so even if your computer is generating a mass mailing for you, give each letter a 'hand-typed' look.

Maybe this sounds too rigid. You're a musician, after all, and not a business tycoon, so why should you conform to someone else's standards? When you're seeking publicity, you'll do better to play by established rules, and with business correspondence that means one thing: type it.

Business Letter Style

Perhaps the simplest, though not the only, format for business letters is the *full block* style, in which everything is lined up with the left margin and no paragraphs are indented.

MARY MCCORMACK

123 DUCK LANE, BATH, AVON, BA5 7NR

17 September 1990

Mr. Greg Stoddard, Manager
Upper Crust Club
123 Highbrow Crescent
Bath
Avon BA1 2CD

Dear Mr. Stoddard

I know you're busy, but I'd like to take a moment of your time to
introduce myself.

I'm a pianist specializing in light music, and have
just moved from London to Bath. While in London, I
worked regularly as a solo artist and with combos, at several
well-established clubs.

I sing, know hundreds of tunes, and get along well with
club 'regulars' and I'd like to work for you.

In the next week or so, I'll call your secretary for a three-minute
appointment to meet you. I'd like to say "hello", and leave a
demo tape and some publicity material.

I look forward to the opportunity of working with you.

Thank you.

Yours sincerely

Mary McCormack

Mary McCormack

P.S. My speciality is remembering the favourite tunes of club
regulars. I'm proud of my memory, and rarely forget a face, name
or special request. Audiences seem to appreciate this trait.
Hope I can demonstrate it for you.

What has Mary accomplished with this letter? Some observations:

- She called the club to get the manager's name, the club's address and postal code. She checked his title, and the spelling of 'Stoddard.'
- She comes right to the point in the first sentence, " . . . I'd like to introduce myself."
- She blows her own horn without overtly bragging, " . . . I know hundreds of tunes . . ."
- The phrase, " . . . I get along well with club 'regulars' shows that she understands the importance of personal rapport with the audience.
- She follows business protocol when she says she'll call in advance for an appointment. And she shows respect for Mr. Stoddard's time by mentioning a three-minute visit.
- She uses "Yours sincerely" because it is the most popular form of close. She could have used "Yours truly" or "Cordially."
- She uses a postscript because she knows that is the most read part of any letter. (Notice that the advertising letters you get *always* include a postscript to add emphasis.) Here, the P.S. repeats the idea that Mary is interested in the club regulars, and implies that she would be a popular addition to the club.
- Mary clips one of her business cards to the letter, but she doesn't include a brochure at this point since she's planning a personal sales call within a week. She'll personally deliver the brochure and demo tape for more impact. (We'll cover sales calls in Chapter Fifteen.)
- The letter is neatly typed in a standard business style.

What Do You Want To Say?

Business letters are time-savers, and should be brief and to the point. Your time is valuable, and so is that of your clients and prospective clients. Don't beat about the bush. There's no need to be verbose, vague, wordy or evasive. The best approach for writing a business letter is to come right out and say what you mean. Even in a letter of complaint, though, always be polite.

Are you writing to introduce yourself? Follow Mary's approach, and say, "I'd like to introduce myself." Are you writing for an appointment? Don't make the reader guess what you're after. Say, "I'd like to set up an appointment to show you how my band can increase the popularity of the Chez Nous club."

Is this a letter of confirmation? Spell out the details as clearly as you can. In such a letter, *always* note the day as well as the date, in case the client doesn't have a calendar handy. "Joe's Band will play on Friday, May 13th, 1988, from 6.00 to 9.00 p.m." Maybe the client really wants you for Saturday, and was confused about when the 13th will be. Writing "Friday" will catch the error before it catches you.

The Unpleasant Truth

Are you writing about an unpleasant subject – an overdue bill, a broken contract, an unsatisfactory performance? Don't be nasty or ugly (which could even get you into legal trouble), but make your point in a business-like way.

"I'm writing to request payment for our performance at your company function six weeks ago. While I realise that the cheque must be issued through your usual procedures, let me point out that you promised payment within two weeks, and that we have been very patient. Please advise when we may expect a cheque."

Or, "I'm truly sorry, Mrs. Jones, that your daughter felt she had to cancel her wedding on the morning of the ceremony, and I know that you've had a traumatic week, but I must point out that our contract does not allow cancellations on the day of the performance. Unfortunately, we had turned down several other jobs for that Saturday, and we must insist on full payment as per terms of the contract. I'm sure you realise that Saturday nights are our prime time."

How does this help your publicity goals? By being business-like in all your dealings – pleasant and otherwise – your reputation will be enhanced. Your clients will be impressed by your professional approach in this unmusical aspect of your career.

What if an engagement was unsuccessful, and your band really was at fault? Perhaps you'd need to offer an adjustment in your fee, but at least a well-phrased letter of apology shows that you care – and helps mend fences. You can't afford unhappy clients.

So, say "I'm sorry about our drummer knocking over the wedding cake, Mrs. Jones. He tripped on the edge of the dance floor and instinctively reached out for support. It's unfortunate that the cake was within his reach, though in years to come I hope the pictures of him lying amid the fallen cake may be cause for amusement rather than anger."

Face up to problems, and be sincere with your apology – even humorous if it's appropriate. Anger or defensiveness, even when justified, is usually counter-productive.

Form Letters Save Time
In the right situation, forms and pre-printed contracts will save time and probably make communication easier, but don't substitute a form for a real live letter. Use forms when a standard, repetitious kind of information is required, design it with your publicity objectives in mind, and make it simple to use.

If you require a legally binding contract, consult a lawyer or use an accepted, tested form. If you're comfortable, however, with a less legalistic kind of communication, just devise a simple form that includes all the pertinent data for your kind of music. Your goal is to save time – yours and the client's – and reduce the chances for a communication error.

If a client won't pay, will such a contract help you in a small claims court? Again, consult a lawyer about the exact form you've devised, but the truth is that in such a situation you may be out of luck, with or without a contract. Sometimes it's just not worth the effort to collect the money, and you'll have to just write it off as a bad debt. If a club goes out of business, there may not be any assets for you to claim, or money to pay your bill. A clear, well-written contract, or confirmation letter, however, will help you make your case.

Of course, you'll print the form on your letterhead, or add your logo to the top or bottom of the page, but also consider having your contract *typeset*, to look extra good. You can pattern the form after a letter, a memo or a contract. Even though the purpose here is to get detailed information in print, you should take care that your professional image is enhanced. You can do this by asking for some kind of specific information that shows your interest in this particular client, and by stating your requirements more like *requests* than demands. Read the sample confirmation agreement on page 125. Notice, particularly, the phrasing of the first three paragraphs. The band-leader is really saying:

1. We charge extra if the piano you provide isn't tuned.
2. We charge extra if we must unexpectedly change locations during a job.
3. We probably charge extra for early set-ups.

But rather than make such demanding-sounding statements, he phrases them so the client doesn't feel insulted.

If you choose to use a form like this one, tailor it to your own kind of music. Make it as handsome as you can by applying the same design principles you used in preparing your other printed material – be sure that the image conveyed is that of a successful professional.

If you have unusual requirements (large space, power or lighting needs, for example) attach a rider listing exactly what you need. But if your needs can be included on one sheet, try to phrase them diplomatically, so the client won't feel that you're making difficult demands. Rock stars are well-known for attaching contract riders specifying everything down to the brand of soft drinks that must be provided. Remember, though, that celebrities can make demands that the rest of us shouldn't try.

Special requirements: We need access to the Plantation room at least an hour, and preferably two, before the function begins. Stage must be 12 by 20 feet. We provide keyboards and sound equipment.

Comments: Company will advise of exact schedule for evening, and will provide a script for the awards music, etc.

Signed _____

Joe Jones, Band-leader
123 St. Leonard's Road
Bristol BS6 7NR
(0272) 345 6789

Client's Signature _____

Company _____

Address _____

City _____

Telephone, office _____

home _____

"Thank You"

There's an old saying that the most powerful words in the English language are "please" and "thank you." It may be true.

123 St. Leonard's Road, Bristol BS6 7NR

Dear Mr. Harvey,

Thank you for hiring Joe's Band to play at your forthcoming function. We are interested in working with you to be sure that this event meets your needs and expectations.

Please take a moment to check all the information below. The smallest details are important, so if there is any discrepancy, or if you have additional requirements, please let us know.

Over the years we've found that the following concerns will help your affair enjoy the best possible music with the least possible confusion.

1. If you are providing a piano, your music will sound much better if the instrument is in tune and good playing condition. If it's not, we'll bring in an electric piano and add a £25 carriage fee.

2. If an unexpected move is required during the course of an engagement it could disrupt your party because our equipment takes time to break down and set up. Should such a move be necessary, additional carriage fees of £25 each for the drummer and keyboardist and £7.50 for every other band member, will apply. We would like to work with you to plan in advance the best location for the band so such moves won't be needed.

3. We always arrive at least an hour before each performance. This gives us ample time to set up our equipment. If an earlier set-up is required, there may be an extra charge for the time involved. We'll gladly work with you to make the logistics of your engagement as smooth as possible.

4. Should you have to cancel this affair, we'll refund the deposit if cancellation is 60 days or more in advance. For cancellations less than 60 days in advance, the deposit is forfeited, unless we are able to book another engagement, in which case we will refund your deposit. If an engagement is cancelled two weeks or less before the event, the entire amount of the contracted price will be due. This does not apply to cancellations due to bad weather when schools and businesses are also closed.

Date of engagement: Thursday, November 9, 1989
Time: 8.00 – 11.00 pm
Place: Plantation Ballroom, Hilton Inn, Northampton
Type of function: Dinner/Show/Dance music for company dinner
Name of band: Joe's Band
Number of musicians in band: 6, including vocalist
Dress: Formal
Agreed fee: £1,500, plus four hotel rooms (doubles)
Deposit of £500 required
Balance of £1,000 is due: at conclusion of engagement
Overtime to be billed at: pro-rata per half-hour

People like to be appreciated for doing a good job, or thanked for spending their money. Since that basic fact of human nature isn't likely to change, get in the habit of sending short thank-you notes.

What if you're a macho guitar player whose band has a mean, masculine image? Should *you* send a thank-you note? Certainly. It doesn't have to be on pink, scented, floral-design note-paper. Match it to your own style.

Further, the thank-you message doesn't even need to be a full-sized letter. A short note works just as well. In fact, you might produce a smaller letterhead to use just for such short notes.

And, unlike business letters, thank-you notes don't have to be typewritten, particularly when you're addressing individuals. Just make sure your handwriting is legible.

Joe's Band
123 St. Leonard's Road, Bristol BS6 7NR

May 12, 1999

Dear Mrs. Bowen,

Thanks for using our band at Jane's wedding reception last Saturday night. We really enjoyed being part of your family's festivities.

We especially liked the serious dancing at the end of the party. Those pictures of the groom doing the "alligator" will probably become family heirlooms.

Thanks again.

Joe Jones

What do you say in a thank-you note? Not much. Thank the client for using your music and mention some aspect of the engagement to personalise the note. That's all.

That's all it takes to show the client that you appreciate her business. Such a thank-you note softens the impact of an invoice if you're sending one, and puts your name, again, before the client. Clip a business card to the note, too; if your music was really good and the party was a success, the client will be more likely than ever to save your card.

Sending thank-you notes is just plain courtesy. It's also good business; thank-you notes continue to sell your music after the engagement is over. There may be another job on the horizon, and the client's friends and associates will certainly need your services sometime. Don't let that client forget who you are.

It's Not 'Junk Mail' When You Send It

A great way to keep your name before those *affect communities* you listed in Chapter Two is to use *direct mail*. You can send postcards, flyers, form letters, or even your own newsletter or demo tapes, to tell people where you're playing and what you're doing.

Remember, client indifference is a fact of life, and you must constantly work to keep your name, and your music, in their minds. Frequent mailings remind them that you're still around.

If you carefully select your target audiences, mailings can be extremely effective publicity tools – and they're not really very expensive when compared with other kinds of advertising. (Of course, postage like other business costs, is tax-deductible, so save all receipts.)

Mailing Lists

In advertising and publicity, direct mail is big business. Large list companies provide mailing lists targeted to incredibly precise audiences – 40-year-old men who like jazz, drive Range Rovers, and live in affluent neighbourhoods, for example. Huge catalogues of available mailing lists are published, and the names of virtually any interest group imaginable are for sale.

You won't *buy* the mailing lists you see, however. You'll *compile* them yourself, and you may have only 10 or 15 names on one list and 80 or a 100 on another, rather than the tens of thousands used by advertising professionals. No matter what the size of your list, you'll get helpful impact from each mailing.

You'll probably find it useful to develop and maintain at least three different lists. First will be a list of regular clients – those who frequently hire you. If your band plays a circuit of 10 different hotel lounges, you'll begin with 10 managers on your list. If you play convention work in a large city, you may have 30 or 40 names of booking agents and convention planners. If you play weddings, your list will include wedding planners, photographers, florists, caterers, as well as agents.

The second compilation you'll need is the *friends of the band* list that helps you keep track of people who like your music. If you play in a club, restaurant, or hotel there will be regular customers – perhaps even fans of yours – who should be kept up to date on where you're playing and what you're doing. Keep a mailing list, and you can keep them posted.

How do you build your 'fan' mailing list? One good way is to distribute cards such as this each time you play. People who like your music fill out the cards, and you add them to your list. It's a simple but effective tool.

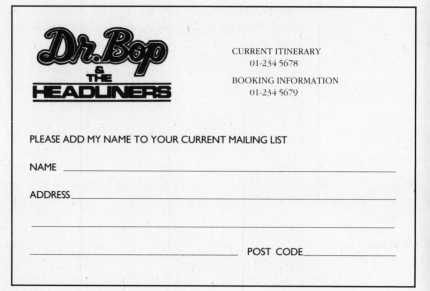

A third list, which you're already keeping, is your *media contacts* compilation. You'll send out press releases and announcements of interest to the press, and a mailing list will expedite the process.

Publicity practice

Start researching a *client list*, including addresses, of all those clients who should know about your music. Include those for whom you've already worked, as well as those who haven't booked you yet. Start with the names you know, and use the Yellow Pages for more listings. There is a thorough discussion of locating such clients in *Profit From Your Music* (Omnibus Press, 1989), by the present author.

Next, start a list of all your loyal fans. When you talk to people in the club or see the same faces each week, ask for their cards, or get their names and addresses. Perhaps you should keep a note-pad for this purpose at the bandstand, or by the cashier, or at the table where you sell T-shirts and tapes. Add these to your *friends of the band* list and keep them updated about where you're playing. You could distribute pre-printed (but not stamped) postcards at the clubs where you play, with the copy "Please add my name to your mailing list so I'll always know where to find Joe's Band."

You should already have a *media contacts list* that you can use for sending out press releases and announcements.

Keep your mailing lists active – add and delete names as people come and go. Using direct mail is easy, but its effectiveness depends on the quality of your lists, so always be on the look-out for potential clients and fans who should be kept informed.

Remember, you don't have to *know* the people on your list, so if you read a newspaper article about a potential new client, go ahead and add her name. Look the address up in the phone book, or call her office to get the proper information.

Nuts and Bolts of Direct Mail

If your mailing isn't too large, use first-class post for simplicity, impact and reliability. First-class post is delivered promptly, and some researchers say that it makes the best impression.

If you expect to mail in very large volume though, you could benefit from the less expensive *bulk mail* rates. Currently, if each posting exceeds 4,000 items, you are eligible for discounts under the Post Office's Mail Sort scheme. Discounts range from around eight to 25 percent off the standard rate, depending on how much 'pre-sorting' of letters into postal districts you are prepared to do. Additionally, pricing is done on a 'straight line' basis, which means, in effect, that if your item weighs just over the standard letter weight, you will pay just over the standard letter price, rather than going up to the next threshold level on the scale of charges.

Producing a Mailing

Who has time to do all that work? You're too busy to spend all day typing addresses each time you have an announcement about your music.

Relax. You shouldn't have to type names and addresses more than once. Modern office technology has made mailing easy. You can use master labels and a photocopy machine or you can use a computer.

The easiest way, if you already have a computer, is to let a mail-merge programme do the work for you. Even the most inexpensive computers can run mail-merge programmes that alphabetise lists, make address changes easy, and print labels in correct sequence. A computer will even let you produce specialised sub-category lists (such as clients who've hired you more than twice, or within the past year, or whatever criteria you want to use).

If you don't have a computer, don't worry. Rather than type each address laboriously onto each envelope, you'll use address labels that can be duplicated on photocopy machines.

You can type as many masters as you need for each list. When it's time for a mailing, simply use a photocopier to run off the self-adhesive labels, and stick them onto each item. It's easy.

What to Mail

Use your mailing lists to keep clients and audiences up-to-date about all your musical activities. When your band opens at a new club, send postcards to everyone on your fan list. You can probably talk the club manager into paying for this mailing, since he'll benefit from larger crowds.

Why not design your own card for more impact? As long as it meets the Post Office's minimum size requirements (100mm x 70mm), you can be as creative as you wish. Your printer will turn your camera-ready copy into an inexpensive and effective mailing piece – including your photo if you wish. Adding a photo does cost a little more, since the printer will charge a few pounds to screen the picture.

Keep your name before agents and regular clients by sending them frequent updates. You could simply send your brochure out a couple of times a year, or you might prepare a different flyer or circular for each mailing. Each regular mailing should bring you more benefit than it costs to produce – though you could overdo it and reach the point of diminishing return. Keep track of results by asking booking clients if they got your flyer.

If yours is a large organisation like an orchestra or a recording studio, you might even produce your own newsletter. Include news of what you've done – concerts, recitals, recordings, new equipment, new repertoire, visiting soloists, fund-raising events, parties, or anything else that might interest your clients. Producing a newsletter, however, is work, so you should have a committee, if possible, to assist in writing, lay-out, printing and distribution. Perhaps a quarterly or twice-yearly newsletter would be effective – and it would help avoid constant deadlines.

If it's appropriate for your kind of music, send regular schedules of available (or not-available) dates to clients who need such timely information – booking agents, party planners, club owners, concert promoters, and, of course, loyal fans. Monthly mailings aren't difficult to do, and your clients will appreciate your business-like approach.

More About Direct Mail

There are many excellent books about direct mail techniques, and extensive research helps advertisers increase response. Here are a few ideas to make your mailings more effective.

Use a teaser on the envelope. How can you be sure the envelope gets opened in the first place? Many professional mailers use questions, statements or illustrations to arouse curiosity. "For a Good Time, Call . . . " Or, "What has ten legs, two horns, and guarantees a good time?" You can type the teaser, have it printed on the envelope, or have your message printed on brightly coloured stickers or labels. Or maybe your logo on the envelope will be the only message you need.

Combine a letter with your circular to increase response. Add either a form letter or a personal one to supplement the message in your brochure. (Personal letters, however, require first-class postage). Remember that most direct mail copy-writers believe that the P.S. is the strongest part of a letter.

Plan your mailing date. If you're interested in booking Christmas jobs for your band, do your first mailing in June and follow up in September. Use a strong teaser to get their attention – perhaps "Christmas in June?" or "For best results, book now, play later." Plan far ahead – your clients do.

Also think about when you want your mail received. Monday and Friday are the busiest posting days; Tuesday is the slowest. January is the busiest mail-order month, when letter-boxes are flooded with catalogues and solicitations. Time your mailing, if possible, to arrive on a slow mail day so it will have a better chance of being noticed. First-class mail is the only category that can dependably be planned this way.

Use first-class mail wisely. Emphasise that you're spending the extra postage by stamping "First Class Mail" on the envelope. This will help distinguish your envelope from the mass of bulk-rate advertisements. And use *commemorative stamps*, which cost no more, but are (usually) larger, more colourful, and more likely to draw attention to the first-class treatment you've given this letter.

Do quickie mailings for special events. When the Sheer Energy band (remember the press release in Chapter Eleven?) schedules its final 'Stars of Tomorrow' TV show, it should send out postcards to all clients and friends – and press releases, of course, to all media contacts. When your band plays an important gig, publicise the event with a postcard blitz.

Also do special mailings to celebrate successes. If the Sheer Energy band wins its contest, there should be a "thanks for your support" mailing. If you get a flattering letter of thanks from the company chairman, or the mother of a bride, or a club owner, incorporate it into a special mailing called "Here's what they're saying about us . . ."

Write On!

Writing letters takes time. It forces you to sit down and think carefully about what you want to say. Because of that care, however, a letter can be a potent force, and a very useful part of your publicity programme. Help your letters work hard for you. Give them a finished, neat appearance, and you'll look like the successful professional you are.

Who else but the post office will deliver your brochure, with a cover letter, to a client across town – or across the country – at such a small cost? Let the postal employees do the walking for you, and keep them busy doing it.

CHAPTER FIFTEEN

SELLING, MEETINGS AND PRESENTATIONS

By now you've developed lots of ways to publicise your musical activities. The time comes, however, when you must get out of the house and actually face potential clients. Someone's got to tell them – face-to-face – about the band, orchestra or show you've produced. It might as well be you.

If you're already rich and famous, you'll have a staff of agents and managers who book jobs for you. The rest of us, however, have to do it ourselves. "Wait a minute," you say. "I'm certainly interested in publicising my music, but I'm not a salesman. I don't mind playing in front of big audiences, but I'd really be nervous talking about myself to clients. Is this really necessary?"

Yes, it is. Dealing directly with clients, whether on the phone or in a face-to-face committee meeting, is crucial to your career. Your publicity efforts have already started the process; now you can complete it by booking some jobs.

Publicity, after all, isn't just paper and photographs. It's also how you act, what you say, and how you're perceived. Good results come from good face-to-face meetings just as much as from good press releases. Your letters and printed material have been working hard for you, selling your music at a distance. This chapter deals with how to sell it in person.

"I'm not a salesman," you may still be thinking. Of course, you're a musician who's worked for years perfecting your art. Your goal is to play the kind of music you want to play – and get paid for it. (If you don't care about getting paid, don't worry about this chapter – or this book. Your music is a hobby, not a profession.)

All the publicity ideas described so far, from business card design to feature articles, are geared toward raising your recognition level and giving you the status of a successful musician. All that work, however, has one ultimate goal – getting you hired to perform. All your publicity efforts ultimately lead to this point of contact with potential clients.

Here, in a nutshell, are the steps to follow in selling your music. First, locate potential clients and contact them. Use the techniques discussed in *Profit From Your Music* to develop a client list from past engagements, referrals, and brainstorming about the kind of prospects who'd *need* your kind of music. Use the Yellow Pages and your experience to create as long a list as possible of those who might hire you. Remember, the more prospects, the more jobs.

Once you've located these potential clients, let them know who you are. Write letters of introduction. Tell them, as Mary did in Chapter Fourteen, that you'll be calling on them soon to talk about your music. Send enough promotional material to warm them up, but save some – perhaps your demo tape and letters of recommendation – to deliver, or demonstrate, in person.

Prepare for the sales call by thinking about your music from the client's point of view. Go back to the list of advantages you developed for your brochure, and *personalise* them in your mind as you think about your music and this particular client. After all, why should he hire you, and not Band *X*? Be sure you're convincing. Practise the sales pitch until you know it backwards and forwards and are confident of what you'll say.

Get a friend to play the client's part in practice sales sessions. They should ask you hard questions, because the client will. "Well, Joe, your band sounds pretty good, but we're running on a tight budget this year. Why should we pay you £500 when we can get another band for £300?"

If you prepare in advance and are confident of the quality of your music, hard questions won't be difficult – they'll just give you the chance to tell another aspect of your story.

Now, let's look at how to act when making the sales call itself.

The Sales Call

Before the call, make an appointment. If you've written to introduce yourself, you already have an advantage – the prospective client knows who you are. If there's not time for a letter, call ahead for an appointment.

Call the client's office and ask to speak to her. Often you'll have to deal with a secretary who carefully shields her boss from unwanted calls. That's why a letter will help – it will get your name known, show you're a professional, and demonstrate that you know business protocol and won't waste valuable time.

Speak clearly, a little more slowly than usual, and confidently when you call. "Hello. This is Joe Jones. I'd like to speak to Ms. Smith, please."

The secretary will probably ask what company you're with, and you should have an answer ready. If you have a business name, use it – or just confidently say why you're calling. "I'm with 'Joe's Band' and I'm calling about music for your Christmas party. I understand that Ms. Smith is the person in charge this year."

The secretary's job is to guard her boss's time by not letting you through. Your job is to be polite but persistent. You're actually doing Ms. Smith a favour by telling her about your terrific band, so don't give up.

Never be rude. No matter what the provocation, don't get angry. Sooner or later you are bound to encounter arrogant, stupid or abrasive secretaries, prospects or clients. Maybe even a few musicians will be less than perfect. Resist the urge to tell them the truth about their abilities – just keep a smile in your voice and be business-like. Everything you say can directly affect your reputation.

You: "Hello. This is Joe Jones. May I speak to Ms. Smith?"

Secretary: "What company are you with, Mr. Jones?"

You: "I'm with 'Joe's Band,' and I'm calling about music for your Christmas party. I understand that Ms. Smith is the person in charge this year."

Secretary: "Well, she won't start planning the party until November, and she's much too busy to talk to musicians. My son's band, 'The Electric Amplifiers,' will probably play for our party, anyway."

Here's where you'll have to remember that *everyone you deal with is important*. Word-of-mouth is the strongest kind of publicity, and making anyone angry is counter-productive. Instead of telling this secretary what you think, be polite – even friendly or humorous if you can – and persist in your request for a short meeting.

You: "Well, I'm sure your son's band is terrific, and I'll listen out for them. Our band specialises in corporate functions, and we played seventeen company parties last December. We'd like to work for you, since we've heard good things about Apex Industries, but December is beginning to fill up. All I need is five minutes to drop some material by, and meet Ms. Smith. How would next Friday morning be?"

You may have to keep trying for days, or longer. You may have to write letters. But if you're persistent, you'll eventually get to see Ms. Smith.

The Office Visit
Appearance is important to business-people, and many of them scrutinise clothes and personal grooming. An old sales cliché says, "You never get a second chance to make a good first impression."

When planning a sales call or presentation, then, try to dress the way your clients dress. If they wear three-piece suits, you should too, if possible. Don't wear jeans or glitzy, show-biz-looking clothes. And don't make sales calls with your shirt unbuttoned to show your collection of gold chains, either.

You may think ICI's dress code is silly – but when you're selling music to ICI how much chance will you have if you wear jeans to a presentation? Be realistic and play by their rules.

Research shows that the way you dress directly affects your success in the business world. You may not want to study the subtle power implications of charcoal versus dark blue suits, but you should pay attention to how you look, and how you're perceived.

So, for sales calls and meetings wear conservative business clothes and be neat and well-groomed. This includes fingernails, breath, hair and polished shoes. (Suits don't go well with trainers – forget the Woody Allen look when you're making business meetings.)

Always be on time. Leave home early enough to deal with traffic, possibly get lost, and find a parking space. The slickest publicity in the world won't help you if the client doesn't think you're trustworthy. Lots of musicians are pretty casual about time; the business world isn't.

Similarly, don't be too early – you'll seem over-eager and too anxious. If you get to the building 20 minutes before your appointment, find the cafeteria and have a cup of coffee. Use the 20 minutes to check over your proposal and practise your sales pitch. Then stop by the cloakroom to be sure your hair and clothes are neat.

Carry your publicity material in a briefcase if you have one, or in a folder or large envelope. It doesn't hurt to carry a newspaper with you in case you have to wait; you'll project a better image if you're catching up on the news than if you're staring into space.

Confidence is crucial in making calls. When you enter the outer office, smile at the secretary and say "Hi. I'm Joe Jones, and I have an appointment to see Ms. Smith at nine fifteen.'' Don't make her guess who you are or what you want. Don't mumble, and don't let fancy office furnishings intimidate you.

When Ms. Smith comes in, stand up, smile, introduce yourself clearly, and shake hands. *You must appear confident, and at ease.* The best way to attain confidence is to believe in your product and be comfortable with your presentation. Practice is the answer.

If you're nervous about meeting clients, remember this: the people you are calling on *need* music. You've identified that fact. And they're going to book someone, some band, to do the job. It might as well be you. In fact, it *should* be you because your music is the best. (If you're not convinced that it is, go back and rehearse until you're a believer.)

When you're in the prospective client's office, don't sit down until you're invited to. Take a minute to talk about the weather, or whatever small-talk seems natural, then get right to your presentation. Make it simple and clear, but don't rush. Ask lots of questions to be sure you're going in the right direction.

Try to maintain a professional, friendly attitude. Don't be a pest, and be sensitive to the client's time; if she glances at her watch, it's time to finish your presentation. And never talk negatively about other musicians. If you say "Our band is much better than Band *X* because our vocalist sings in tune,'' chances are that the vocalist in Band *X* is the client's daughter. It's much safer to stick to business.

Similarly, off-colour stories and jokes have no place in these discussions. While you may be trying to relate as 'one of the guys,' you may offend someone without knowing it. You'll make a better impression if you're pleasant and business-like.

Know exactly what your prices are for different situations, and how much you'll give up to get the job. You'll often do better in the long run if you refuse to work below your own bottom line; sometimes a client just can't afford you. Decide in advance how far, if at all, you'll bargain. One useful idea is to insist that any price concession be matched by a reduction in hours, in size of the band, or be made up another way – meals and rooms to be provided, for instance.

If a prospective client comes up with a question that you can't answer, just say, "I'll have to work up an answer for you on that one, and I'll call you with it first thing in the morning.'' In a sales call, don't promise anything that you can't deliver or that will cause trouble later. Don't let yourself be swept away by the possibility of booking a job.

Are You Listening?

While meeting a prospective client, listen to what he's saying. In fact, learn to listen between the lines for extra information. For example, if he's planning a four-day sales meeting at the Ritz, and is flying in his entire national sales staff, you can assume that he's not counting pennies. He's more interested in quality than in cutting costs.

On the other hand, if he mentions that this year's meeting is much smaller than last year's and is being held in the company boardroom rather than at the Ritz, you should be sensitive to his concerns about expenses. He may not *tell* you directly, but if you listen carefully you'll know that expenditure is being closely monitored. Such clues will help you tailor your proposal to his requirements, and such awareness helps guarantee success.

Your publicity material points out that you're sensitive to clients' needs. Meeting the client gives you a chance to prove it. If you listen to what's on his mind, you'll be able to offer genuine help, and make yourself indispensable.

When you've told your story, *ask for the booking* (called the *close* by professional salesmen). Don't make the client wonder why you're wasting his time. Present your ideas, tell him how much you'll charge, put a contract form on his desk, and say "Shouldn't we go ahead and fill out this confirmation now, so you'll be sure of having the music you need?"

When you leave his office, make notes on what you proposed, how he reacted, when to call again, and any personal characteristics you should remember. Write a thank-you letter whether or not you got a booking. Plan follow-up letters or visits, and mark the calendar to remind you.

Presentations Sometimes, you'll need to make official presentations to a prospective client – perhaps even to a committee. Such a presentation is a formal sales meeting, and it gives you the opportunity to publicise your music to several people at one time.

In a one-to-one sales call you'll usually just talk naturally with the client, but in a presentation you may need to prepare a script. Don't write a speech, word for word, to get through a presentation, but an outline of your major points will help keep you on track.

First, research the job you want to book. Find out as much as you can about it – for instance, who played it last year, how many hours were involved each day, how much rehearsal time is required, and so on. Find out, if you can, what the musicians were paid last year.

More important, find out who the audience will be. Will your show be aimed toward middle-aged tourists or teenagers? Will it be a dinner show, or a late evening's entertainment?

How do you get this information? Ask around. Ask the client what's expected – he'll at least give you the general guidelines. You or your friends probably know someone who was in last year's band, so talk to him (unless you're competing for the job). You could even get information from other employees, such as waiters and waitresses.

Such background information gives you a head start – it keeps you from beginning at point zero. You at least know what's been done – and if it was successful, you can duplicate it. If it was unsuccessful last year, you can offer constructive suggestions for changes.

The Press Kit

For an important presentation, you'll provide complete press kits for each person at the meeting. Tailor the kit to this prospective engagement. Include your brochure, group pictures, pertinent press releases, and photocopies of press cuttings and reviews. Also include copies of thank-you letters from satisfied clients. Include the strongest material *that relates to the presentation you're making*. You might even want to include an audio demo tape in each kit.

So, emphasise relevant experience. If you're trying for an engagement at the new-wave rock club, don't include your wedding and bar mitzvah promo material. And, most people looking for wedding bands won't need to know about your months at the punk rock club. Target the press kit to the needs of each client.

If you're a show band, you'll have a good strong video demo. Take it to the meeting, and be sure that playback equipment will be available – in the right format.

Tell Them Now

Your presentation will be like a little speech. Tell them, simply, what your music can do for them. Remember that business people are results-oriented, always interested in the bottom line. Offer specific, concrete ideas of how your music will help them meet their objectives. Plan ahead and work hard (brainstorming helps) to come up with real-life situations and actual examples – concrete suggestions make your presentation much more effective.

Be specific. "The manager at the Golden Nugget told us that he sold more drinks when we played than the weeks before or after, and he attributed that to our fast-paced, upbeat show." You're demonstrating here that you know what's important to the management team and that you'll be interested in working with them.

Show them, with the demo tape if possible, what you're talking about. Prepare them for viewing your demo by briefly pointing out your special strengths – "Notice the pacing, if you will. Once we start the show, the momentum builds to a powerful finish that leaves the audience calling for more." Offer to leave the video behind for further viewing. (If you only have an audio tape, playing it during the presentation could cause a boring lull, so you may prefer to leave tapes for the clients to listen to at their leisure.)

Tell them *again* how you'll help them. It won't hurt to repeat a bit – salespeople and preachers constantly repeat to be sure the point is being made. Prepare for this by using the Publicity Practice list from Chapter Five, where you brainstormed the ways you could meet a client's needs. Review the list, and apply those ideas to this presentation. Does the client want sophistication, a show, a rowdy good time, an exciting sales meeting, or music for a theme party? The more you can relate your music to the client's needs, the better your chances of being hired.

Emphasise your experience. Refer to other, similar jobs you've done. Drop a few names, if you have them to drop. "Our band spent last summer in Brighton, working in cabaret at the Golden Nugget and Snoots. We opened for a different 'name' act each week, and we never felt that we were out-classed by all that top-flight entertainment."

Make your presentation short and simple. Look at your audience, smile, speak clearly. Don't think that you should use big words because you're in a formal setting – be as natural as you can. And stay away from musical jargon and 'inside' cleverness.

End your presentation by passing out press kits to each member of the committee. Tell them, as you hand out the material, what's inside, and emphasise that each kit contains its own demo tape. Many professional sales-people think it's a bad idea to hand out your material *before* the presentation because committee members will tend to look at your material rather than listen to your remarks.

Thank them for coming, tell them that you look forward to working with them, and leave. Never say that you need this job – even if you do. Remember, they care about *themselves*, not about you.

Should you discuss money at the first presentation? You should be prepared to, in detail, but you should take your cue from the clients. At the initial meeting they may simply want to meet you and get your ideas. Money talk can come later. Find out when they'll make their decisions, and check back with your contact then. If you're working on a really big account, you may schedule another meeting. If it's a smaller job you're after, you can probably follow up by telephone and send the contract by post. In any case, don't forget the thank-you note.

To Close

Sales meetings and presentations give you a chance to put your publicity material and skills to practical use, to try them out on the ultimate consumer of your music.

If you've done a good job preparing these tools, you'll find that they reinforce your image as a competent professional. From the time she first sees your letterhead, the prospective client knows that you take your career seriously, and will do a good job for her.

In fact, your publicity material will have a *synergising* effect in which the results are greater than the sum of the parts – everything works together to create good publicity, which generates more publicity, which generates even more.

As a musician, you're used to being on stage. Nervousness is probably a thing of the past – you can perform before thousands without flinching. If you look at your sales meetings and presentations the same way – as performances – you may be surprised at how much you enjoy them.

After all, you can be on stage in more than one way – and a virtuoso sales performance can bring you as much satisfaction as a perfectly executed solo. The big difference is that instead of applause from the audience, your sales performance is rewarded with a contract.

CHAPTER SIXTEEN

PEOPLE AND PUBLICITY

Is publicity worth all the effort? Does it really work?

A famous story among public relations professionals tells how the right kind of publicity helped make Bing Crosby a superstar. Many powerful people in the entertainment industry felt that his popularity would be limited to women. They thought he was too much a crooner to appeal to men.

Crosby's publicity people looked for a hook that would broaden his appeal – and they found it in the masculine sport of horse-racing. Soon, stories appeared in newspapers and magazines about Bing Crosby's interest in racing, his constant visits to the track, and his friendship with jockeys. His show was peppered with race-track jokes, and newspapers carried pictures of Bing at the track.

Did Bing Crosby really like racing? Probably. But his publicist saw this identification as a way to demonstrate that he was a real *macho* character who liked masculine things. His popularity soared.

This is how publicity works. You plot specific ways of getting your message out – whether it's that you're a macho horse-lover, or that your band is the best in town. You use major media – newspapers, radio, magazines – when they're appropriate, but you don't stop there.

Publicity comes from everything you do. Bing Crosby was a singer, but racing provided the publicity hook he needed. You're a musician, but who knows what you'll find useful in blowing your own horn? You can tailor your image just as Bing Crosby's publicity advisors did.

A good understanding of publicity, then, shows you that almost *anything you do* can get you noticed. You aren't limited to the standard publicity approaches we've already discussed. Of course, news and feature stories are wonderful, but don't stop there. The world of good publicity is as wide as you can make it.

We've discussed *hooks* linking your musical event to a larger cause that broadens its appeal. By now you should be finding hooks everywhere, and thinking about the publicity potential of all kinds of activities.

This chapter discusses several very simple, direct ways of creating, or advancing, good publicity. These are down-to-earth ideas. You can start using them *tonight*. You probably won't decide to associate yourself with horse-racing to demonstrate your macho toughness, but you can devise publicity activities to suit your music.

The music business, like most others, is a *people business*. You deal with other musicians, agents, brokers, planners, club owners and audiences. You play for nice folks and boors; you work for gentlemen and jerks. You meet so many people that you'll never remember them all. And you interact with them on many levels. With care, you can turn these daily personal interactions into positive publicity.

Everybody's Talking About Me

Get people talking. *Word-of-mouth* is the strongest and most direct publicity medium of all. In fact, all the publicity you create is really aimed at getting people to talk about you. So work at it.

Talk yourself up. Don't be shy. *Be proud of your profession.* Keep a high profile – wear your band T-shirt around town. When someone asks what you do, don't mumble, "I'm a musician." Say, "I'm the drummer in Joe's Band – the best band around. Maybe you've heard us – but if you haven't, you will." If you don't believe in yourself, why should anyone else?

Ask people to talk about you. When you've done a particularly good job for a business client, for example, ask her to recommend you. Tell your clients, "Please talk about us. Tell your friends how much fun you had at this party. We love it when you make our ears burn."

People will talk about you anyway, so work to make it positive. Be sure your band members all understand that they're sales-people as well as musicians. One sloppy drummer eating at the guests' buffet table, or a horn player who scoffs at a client's request, can do lots of harm to your reputation. Being super-courteous is a good way to inspire positive word-of-mouth publicity.

Work with your band to be sure everyone shares the same goals and ideas. When you're on break at the club, mingle with the audience. Ask for their feedback and requests; let them know you appreciate them. Don't forget to get names and addresses for your fan mailing list.

There's an old publicity cliché, "I don't care what they say about me as long as they spell my name right." You do care what they say – and about the spelling of your name – but your goal is really to *keep them talking*.

Keep Them Talking

Here are a few specific ideas to spread the word:

Offer finder's fees to people whose referrals result in more bookings for your group. Car salesmen and wedding photographers do this all the time. Mention in your thank-you note that you'll pay £15 for each referral that works out. (Some musicians won't feel comfortable with this, and it won't work with corporate clients who might see it as a bribe, but it's a useful technique for many situations.) Many 'casual' engagements depend on a network of people; to book weddings, for example, you could work closely with photographers, caterers, wedding planners and florists – and devise a reciprocal finder's fee arrangement with each of them.

Use your mailing list to send Christmas or New Year's cards. Do it because you really care about your clients – your "best wishes for the coming year" are genuine. And it doesn't hurt to remind them of your existence. (Remember that image without substance won't last, so let your clients know that you honestly appreciate their business and work hard to do a good job for them. Don't let them feel that you're just using them.)

Make yourself a recognised authority. If you're an expert, exploit your knowledge. Work up a speech and present it to associations, conventions – any audience you can find. Talk about music, children, education, history, trends and fads, give demonstrations, show slides or videos – whatever. And publicise your speech, of course.

What else could you do to demonstrate that you're an authority?

Apply to your local education authority to teach an adult education class. These courses are very popular, and your experience and personality will be more important in getting hired than academic credentials. Teaching a class in 'The History of Jazz,' 'Beginning Improvisation,' 'Playing Blues Harmonica,' or 'Rock and Roll Roots' will give you important credibility, enhance your image, and even pay you.

It's not as important that these courses be traditional as that they be interesting. If you have a good idea, prepare a presentation for the director of an adult education department. They're looking for appealing courses that will involve the community and attract students, and you can help.

If you're an expert, you should send your name to the news media in your area for their 'experts file,' as discussed in Chapter Thirteen. When they need a comment, explanation or interview about your area of expertise, they'll call – and you'll get wide exposure. Perhaps a famous jazz trumpet player dies, and you're the local jazz trumpet expert – a local radio station might interview you about his influence. Or perhaps the government has just cut funding for music courses at the local college, and a TV station asks for your reactions. They won't interview you if they don't know that you're an expert.

Be good. Be the best at what you do. Most of your audience, let's face it, will be musically illiterate, but sometimes you'll play for people who recognise quality – and they'll be impressed enough to talk about you. If you're a piano player, don't get lazy on those boring single jobs. Pretend that Oscar Peterson is in the room every night. Who knows – someday he may be. It's easy to forget that quality counts.

Help Others and They'll Help You

There are lots of ways your music can help worthy causes and create good publicity at the same time, so you should be willing to give your music away – sometimes. Develop a policy for donating your music, and stick to it. It's true that you'll get 'exposure' by playing free for this cause or that fund-raising drive, but you can't eat exposure. If you perform for a living, your talent is valuable.

You could easily spend all your time helping all the good causes that exist in every city. Since each important disease has its own fund-raising body, and since many of them sponsor well-publicised society events, you must know how often you can afford to donate your time and music. Decide how many free events you'll play a year. Maybe you'll do one, or two. If you're popular, you'll probably be asked to do 10 or 12 – or more.

It's not inappropriate to think about which donations of your talent will bring you the most good publicity. Ask if you'll be mentioned in the official programme, or if you can get a photograph – or a page – devoted to your music. Find out if you'll be publicised by the organisation through the media.

You can, and should, bargain for publicity in exchange for donating your music. Work with the committee – usually volunteers who may not know much about publicity – in preparing their press releases, brochures and programmes. Provide them with your own bio sheets, photos and background material, and insist that your music be mentioned in their publicity programme.

Always remember what your music is worth, and act accordingly. If your band normally gets £750 for a night, be sure that the charity you're working with knows it. Get written acknowledgement of the amount of your donation for use in filing your income tax return.

Musical ability is a gift and you should be willing to share it. There are so many worthwhile causes, however, that you'll have to make careful choices. You'll find that limiting your donations will, in the end, raise your prestige and gain you more respect.

Cultivate The Personal Touch Develop personal relationships with press people and clients. If you are friendly and naturally like people, this will be easy for you. Everyone appreciates being remembered by name. If you have trouble recalling names and faces, read a book on memory development. Business cards help you remember people if you jot a few facts on the back. You can also keep a small notebook handy to write down bits of personal information. If you read in the paper that your client John Smith has just returned from a skiing holiday in the Italian Alps, make a note to ask him about it next time you see him.

You *are* keeping a cuttings file of interesting publicity ideas, aren't you? There's another simple way you should use clippings – this time to keep your name before your clients. When you see an article about a client, or a client's interest, cut it out and send it to him with a very short note. It shows that you're interested in him and his activities. Thus, if you see an interesting photo essay on skiing in a photographic magazine, cut it out and send it to Mr. Smith. Attach a short note that says simply, "I thought you'd be interested in this." You might even write the message on the back of your business card.

Do the same when you see an article by, or about, clients or contact people. It only takes a moment, and is an excellent way to build relationships while reminding them of your existence. Best of all, it focuses attention on the client's interest – not on you.

Reach Out and Grab Someone

Involve others in your music. You can pull in regulars from your audience, or you can work with local celebrities. For example, say you're looking over the media contacts list you've compiled and you notice that the features editor of your newspaper is an amateur trombone player. Why not invite him to play with your band for a particular event? Perhaps he'll accept, perhaps not, but he'll appreciate – and remember – your invitation.

This idea can be expanded to fit whatever kind of music you do, and can involve all kinds of public figures. It's the old piggyback-publicity idea, and it works. But celebrities are busy – sometimes booked solidly for months ahead. If you'd like to involve a TV sports commentator, say, in judging a dance contest, you'll have to plan ahead. (And, when you have a commitment, write a confirmation letter *immediately*, and follow up with a reminder or two. These people are busy, and you need them more than they need you – so don't let your function be overlooked.)

Is the mayor of your town an amateur conductor? Invite him to conduct the overture at your college orchestra's concert, and publicise the event widely. (It doesn't matter whether he's a good conductor or not – in fact, it could be more interesting and amusing if he's inept – and has a good sense of humour. Edward Heath, the former Prime Minister, was an accomplished amateur conductor and generated lots of publicity for the orchestras he visited; perhaps there's a celebrity 'closet conductor' in your town, too.

Involve a popular TV personality in one of your events. Most television people enjoy the spotlight – many of them, in fact, have sizeable egos. So invite the anchor-woman of the Six o'Clock News to narrate 'Peter and the Wolf,' or to judge an amateur-night singing contest, or to be in the video you're making. She'll probably love the publicity, and her station may well decide to cover the music-related activities of one of their own personalities.

Sports figures are very popular in many cities, and if you know one who has a musical interest, work on a special event to involve him. Maybe the centre-half of the local team writes songs about football. Perhaps you could hold a 'world première' party to introduce his compositions to the public.

The fame and reputation of public personalities will enhance yours, and they will often be happy to work with you on worthwhile projects. If you are involved in a local charity project, work with one – or more – celebrities when planning the entertainment. Perhaps you're playing for a fund-raiser for the homeless in your city. Why not invite a local celebrity to be the evening's MC, judge a dance contest, pick the best costume, or just be the on-stage host to welcome the crowd?

Move Over *ITV*, I'm Forming My Own Network

As you work with more and more people you'll develop friendships that are also business relationships – and you'll realise that most business is done at a personal level. Susan meets you, you get along, and she hires your band. If she doesn't meet you, or doesn't like you, she'll probably hire someone else.

Networking is an old activity with a new name. You're building a network of clients and referral sources anyway, and if you're organised about it you'll get more from – and give more to – your relationships. Always working at meeting new people who need your music will help solve the most basic problem faced by most musicians: finding new clients.

Do what insurance sales-people do. After each sales call, whether they've sold insurance or not, they ask, "Do you know anyone else who would benefit from hearing about my product?" Thus, each sales call leads directly to several more, and the sales-person's base of contacts grows quickly.

You should do the same. After each job, ask your client if there are any business associates or friends who should know about your music. If the client makes suggestions, write them down and ask if you can use his or her name in introducing yourself.

Thus, you can say, "Hello, Mrs. Johnson, I'm Joe, of Joe's Band, and we just played for Mary Bernard's wedding reception last week. Mary told me that your daughter, Helen, is planning a wedding, and suggested that I give you a call to tell you about our band.''

When you use a mutual acquaintance's name your position is strengthened, and the recommendation gives you a boost. Don't neglect, then, to ask for referrals. While you're at it, ask for letters of commendation or thanks from clients who seem especially appreciative of your work. In a short time, you'll have a file bulging with good recommendations that will be very useful in developing more publicity materials.

''Mr. Jones, we've had a great time playing for your company party, and I think your employees enjoyed themselves, too. I wonder if I could ask you a favour? Would you mind writing me a letter of recommendation based on our work for you tonight? We try to keep a file of letters from our clients.'' Mr. Jones, of course, will be glad to dictate that letter. It won't take him very much time, and he'll be flattered that you value his opinion.

Also, after successful jobs ask your clients if you might use their names as references. Let them know that you won't overdo it and have them pestered with lots of phone calls. Often you'll find that a prospective employer needs to talk with a past client or two to feel comfortable about hiring your band.

Keep building a network of satisfied clients. Use your mailing list to stay in touch, and use their influence to build your career.

I'll Trade You . . .

We discussed bartering your music for professional help in Chapter Nine, but this can also be an interesting way to expand your musical influence. You'll be surprised how often people will be willing to trade goods or services for music – and you'll profit by expanding your list of clients, working in more situations, and increasing your network of contacts. Plus, you'll get whatever you've bartered for.

You'll have most success dealing with small businesses and professionals. Large companies won't usually be flexible enough to engage in a barter transaction.

When would you trade your music? And for what? Trade it anytime, for anything. You'll have to be the creative brains behind these transactions, but if you approach it right you can really profit. If you're part of a group, of course, the trade will have to benefit everyone equally.

Does your flat need decorating? Ask your local decorator if he's planning a garden party, house party, anniversary celebration or whatever – and exchange your solo guitar performance for new décor.

Do you need a brochure printed or a photograph taken? Find a printer or photographer whose daughter is getting married, or who is about to throw a 'grand opening party' for his new shop.

Are you ready for a week in the Lake District? Find a small hotel that will trade you a room with meals for a week in return for your music. In cases such as these, a barter may not work out to be equal, and you may require a small payment as well as the room.

Do you buy drum-sticks every time you pass the music shop? Why not arrange with the shop owner for a Saturday afternoon workshop to demonstrate a new line of drums – in return for a year's supply of sticks.

A good use for barter is to fill up slow nights, weeks or months. Do you rarely work on Mondays? Try to arrange your bartered jobs for times when you wouldn't expect to have a paying job. You've gained, without losing anything.

There's no limit to what you can barter. But when you set up such a swap, trade *value for value*. Don't cut your quality just because you aren't getting paid in cash, and insist that your trading partner does the same. A good barter is a 'win/win' situation.

Exploit the publicity angles of bartered jobs just as you would any other engagement. Use each job to locate others, and to add to your file of good publicity material.

These are just some of the ways you'll be able to expand the effects of your publicity by dealing positively with people. Talk it up, help others, show them you're interested, invite them to participate in your events, trade your music, and create a network of contacts.

The benefits of meeting lots of people are very clear. The more people you know, the more people know you. And the more they know you, the more they hire you.

CHAPTER SEVENTEEN

GOOD PUBLICITY IS EVERYWHERE

How many more publicity ideas are there? As many as you can devise – and they certainly aren't all discussed here or in any book. You'll invent better, more useful ideas as you work on your publicity programme.

Here are more ideas, though, that you can use to spread the word about your music. Most of these, in keeping with the idea of avoiding advertising (which costs money) are free, or very low-cost projects. Several of them have been mentioned in earlier chapters – they're included here to remind you, or to expand their value as publicity generators. It will be useful to occasionally re-read this chapter so you won't forget these ideas, or get in a publicity rut. Even after you're a PR expert, there will be lots of avenues you haven't explored, so work at being alert, creative and flexible.

You've already turned your band members into sales-people, and worked on spreading the word about our music through the best of all media – word of mouth. You've worked at involving yourself in the community to elevate your image, and at involving community leaders in your music. What else can you do?

A lot. Turn everything into publicity aids. You can start wherever you are.

Keep Your Publicity Material Handy
Remember the Boy Scout motto, "Be prepared." When you're asked about your music, be prepared to answer in the most effective way you can – with your publicity material. Don't wait a few days and post it – do it now.

Always keep a few complete press kits in your briefcase, instrument case or car. Handing out business cards is good, but when people express an interest in your band, strike while the iron is hot by giving them the requested information – now.

Whether you use fancy presentation folders or simple envelopes, always have a few sets ready to hand out. Include your brochure, photo, a few press releases, photocopies of news stories, and maybe even a demo tape.

If you're playing a private party and the catering manager of the hotel asks about your band – give him the entire press kit. If you're playing a country-club dance and someone enquires about your availability for a wedding reception, give them your high-quality materials.

Being prepared this way will take advantage of a client's interest on the spot. It will impress him that you're efficient and business-like. And the excellence of your publicity material will reinforce your image as a competent professional.

Answering Machines
Does your answering machine actively expand your publicity – or is it just a bland business helper? Make it a publicity tool – have the message tell part of

your story. It needn't be a full-scale 30-second commercial, but it can subtly spread the word. Here are two real-life examples.

The leader of a group called Best Bet uses this message: "Hi. You've reached 123-4567, your best bet for musical entertainment. If you leave your message after the tone, we'll get right back in touch. Thanks for calling."

That's short, and very low-key. The band's name is mentioned naturally, and the message is short. Nevertheless, the caller gets the message that this band is his best bet.

Best Bet's answer is much better than, "Hello. We're using this answering machine to take messages. When you hear the beep, you'll have 30 seconds to leave your message." After all, everyone knows how to leave a messages by now; there's no need to sound like you're reading from the answering machine instruction book.

A guitarist/singer I know always uses song parodies for his phone machine message. His machine allows outgoing messages of various lengths, so he can add the beep when the tune ends. The trick here is to make the words appropriate, and clearly understandable. Such messages are made more effective, too, if the music reaches a logical quitting point just before the beep sounds. Here's an example – a blues:

> Well, I know the phone's ringing,
> But I just ain't around.
> I'm probably playing my guitar
> For some happy folks downtown.
> If you'll leave your name and number
> I'll call you when I can,
> 'Cause I'm your friendly, soulful,
> Rock-and-roll guitar man. (BEEP)

Now that looks silly in print, but it sounds great on the phone, because the music and words work together so well. The message demonstrates his singing, playing – and sense of humour.

Writing clever words and getting the timing to work right, takes practice – but you can do it. And don't use the cheap plastic mike that came with the answering machine if you can find a better one.

If you try this musical approach, keep your message-tune short, and change it frequently. People who call you regularly may not enjoy hearing your 60-second 'Telephone Machine Blues' several times a week.

Use Body Language

Why not wear your message and turn yourself into a walking ad for your music? Your own T-shirt or other imprinted clothing will travel with you and carry your message to everyone you meet. T-shirts are easy to produce, can be creatively designed, are a great advertising/publicity medium, and don't cost much. You can also produce golf shirts, sweatshirts, jackets, caps and visors. After all, you've got to wear something.

Shirts, and other imprintable wearables, are available in all sizes and colours. You design the illustration or copy, and have the shirt *silk-screened* to transfer your art to it. The silk-screening process handles very fine detail and uses inks that are bonded permanently to the fabric. The silk-screen process, from your standpoint, is much like working with a quick-copy printer. You simply provide finished camera-ready artwork, which is transferred to cloth rather than paper.

There is a standard set-up charge for turning your artwork into a film positive, and then into the silk screen. The fee varies, but currently should be in the region of £20. The set-up price is doubled if you want printing on the back, and is charged again for each additional ink colour.

Some printers can print only limited image sizes; others can print across the entire shirt. Remember that people probably won't want to stare at your shirt to get the message, so make the copy simple and the letters large. Maybe your logo by itself will be all you need, or you can come up with a good design using your band's name or even a photo.

To find a silk-screen shirt printer, consult the Yellow Pages under "T-shirt printers," "screen process printers," or "Promotional items." You'll probably be most successful with a small – perhaps one-person – operation. Large T-shirt printers often have high minimum orders, but a smaller operator will be happy to work with you.

Most T-shirt printers have minimum orders of at least two or three dozen shirts. If you are part of a five-piece band, for example, you may not need that many. Explain your situation to the producer – you may be able to have just a few shirts printed, at a higher per-shirt cost. If you have to order the full minimum you could give (or sell) the extras to your fans.

The per-shirt price does drop significantly as you order more shirts. You might pay £3.50 per shirt if you order two dozen, but only £2 each for larger quantities. Shop around, and look at samples of the shirts you're considering. You should be able to get a first-quality cotton/polyester blend that will last well – and look good. In fact, your shirt could be the exact same brand as the expensively imprinted shirts sold in fashionable boutiques.

When ordering large numbers of shirts to be distributed to the public, one rule of thumb is to order twice as many medium and large shirts as small and extra-large ones. Or, if you can take size orders in advance, you'll be sure to get a shirt to fit everyone.

If you're likely to re-order, be sure to tell the T-shirt producer. While the screen probably won't be saved, the film positive will be filed away to await your next order.

Some colours print better on T-shirts than others. Look at samples of the shirt/ink colour combinations you like to be sure that the shirt colour doesn't bleed through. Thus, a light grey shirt with black printing should present no problem, while a bright red shirt might turn white ink into a sickly pink. Get assurances from your printer that the combination you like will work.

While you're dealing with the T-shirt printer, look at the entire line of imprinted items. Would umbrellas with your logo be useful? If you're a country band, how about truck-driver style caps? You can even work with corporate clients to provide shirts specifically made for one single event – "Blag and Grabbit 10th Annual Dinner-Dance" – with, perhaps, your band's picture or logo on the shirt. In such a case, the company would pay for the shirts and give them to its employees and guests – and to the band, of course. Make this suggestion to your corporate contacts when a large, informal party is being planned.

If you can wear your message, and get others to do the same thing, you'll get noticed everywhere you go. Let your shirt do the talking.

Throw a Party

Why not have a party once or twice a year for your friends and business contacts? It needn't be elaborate, and it will give you a chance to enjoy yourself and do some serious networking if you like.

Many musicians, particularly those who work six nights a week in clubs, don't have much social life. You can't go out with friends if you're always working, and it's easy to become isolated. Parties help get you back in circulation.

You could have a music-oriented party, at which your band plays, or you could have a full-scale jam session and invite all your musical friends to sit in. If you're inviting clients and prospects, however, think carefully about whether a jam session would appeal to them – it might seem chaotic, or boring, and actually be counter-productive. Perhaps you'd benefit from a party to present your new demo tape, or introduce your new vocalist or manager.

If you're working in a club, try to talk the manager into letting you use the club's facilities, perhaps on a Sunday afternoon, for your festivities. Perhaps he'll even provide beer and hors d'oeuvres. You could, of course, have the party at your house, or even rent a facility.

Maybe you should plan a one-band showcase and invite only potential clients, business associates and media contacts. If so, be sure to attend carefully to all the details that will make your party a completely positive experience. (And be sure to save all the receipts, since business expenses are tax-deductible.)

Sponsor a band picnic, cricket game, swimming party, snowball fight, jam session, road race, volleyball game, or street dance. If your group can work with another organisation, why not join forces to do something really elaborate – a Halloween party, or theme party that encourages creativity?

When you have a party, no matter what kind it is, try to arrange everything so that your guests have a good time. Don't hit them over the head with your "hire me" message – if they enjoy themselves, that's enough.

Join Forces

Find an organisation to work with – or even sponsor – your group. This approach gives your music more impact, because you are linked with the sponsor's reputation, and you can share its publicity.

Established musical groups – such as professional symphony orchestras – often have corporate sponsors for an entire season, or a series of concerts, as in the case of Du Maurier's sponsorship of the Philharmonia Orchestra.

Corporate sponsors are usually interested in supporting kinds of music that have artistic merit and aren't widely popular or self-supporting. Thus jazz, opera, classical music, chamber music and so on probably have better chances than pop bands for encouraging corporate support.

Regional arts associations often offer grants to worthwhile musical endeavours. You could get a grant to present programmes to schools on jazz, chamber, folk or whatever your speciality is. Or you might secure funding from a research foundation to locate, transcribe and record the indigenous music of ethnic communities represented in your area. Many times, grants are made for decidedly non-commercial projects, so search for worthwhile, even academic ideas that relate to your kind of music.

Corporate sponsors like to work with musicians because they get excellent publicity from these events. Musicians benefit financially, and reap good publicity, too. When a corporate sponsor is paying you to perform weekly concerts in a city park, the company's advertising and public relations staff will work hard to publicise the event – and you.

To locate possible corporate sponsors, think about the largest industries and companies in your area. Are any related in any way to your kind of music? (A beach-wear manufacturer could logically sponsor a series of beach-music parties.) Have any of them done this kind of thing before? A large bank that's sponsored lunch time concerts in a park, for example, would be a good prospect for a similar series in suburban areas. Are any of them notably civic- or arts-minded? Contact their public relations offices with your ideas, and if they're interested, they'll ask for a full presentation. Again, show how the project will benefit *them*.

Test to Learn What Works

Big advertisers use scientific techniques to find out if their advertising and publicity are working. This is called 'testing,' and all smart advertisers do it. You can do the same thing; you'll work more effectively when you know what publicity and advertising efforts work for you.

Watch what others do. If your competitors are getting good publicity, find out how they're doing it, and copy them. Keep your cuttings file active – cut out and save all the articles you see about other musicians and arts groups. Ask yourself, "How did she go about getting that story in the paper? What kind of press release did she send?"

If it's appropriate (that is, if the article isn't about a *direct competitor*), call and ask. "Hello, Susan, I really enjoyed reading that feature story on your innovative piano teaching techniques. I'm trying to expand my class of voice students, and I wonder if you'd mind telling me how that story came to be in the paper?" Most of the time people will be glad to tell you – because most people like to talk about themselves.

Ask clients and prospective clients where they heard of your band. Keep track of their answers. "Referred by Sandy at the Ritz hotel." Or, "Saw flyer at music shop." You'll quickly get a feel for which of your publicity efforts bring the most response, and you'll know to continue or reinforce them.

Go Where the Clients Go

Put your publicity material where it will be seen by the right clients. Often, shop managers will let you leave brochures or flyers at their shops, or they may have a noticeboard where you can display a poster.

If you play for weddings, leave brochures and cards at formal-wear shops, with wedding photographers and florists, and with wedding planners and caterers. Notice that most formal-wear shops display the work of local wedding photographers, and you should distribute your material the same way.

Be innovative. Does the formal-wear shop, or the photographer, use video-taped presentations? If so, arrange to leave one of your tapes for their clients to view.

You may work out a referral fee and agree to pay a commission for jobs you book with the help of these shops. Sometimes this will be appropriate, and sometimes not. Make it clear that you're not trying to buy the business unethically, but are offering the same kind of commission you'd otherwise pay an agent.

Use Unique Printed Material

We've discussed brochures and letterheads, and how to design them. Use the same techniques to devise speciality pieces to promote your music.

Table tents, request cards. If you play in a restaurant or club, why not design your own promotion piece for each table? You could incorporate your logo or a picture of your band. Such pieces can be self-standing triangles, printed on two sides and flat on the bottom, or they can be simple cards to fit the plastic holders that many restaurants use. Of course, you'd need the manager's permission to add promo items to the tables, but why not work with him – and convince him he should pay for the printing? After all, increasing your popularity also increases his business.

If you enjoy taking requests and interacting with the audience, print your own request cards, again with your logo and name prominently displayed. You'll be surprised how many people take such cards home; the publicity is always worth the cost.

Some bands distribute pre-printed postcards to build up their mailing lists. The copy reads: "Yes, I'd like to be the first to know where Joe's Band will be playing next. Add me to your mailing list." Space is then provided for name and address.

Posters are useful in lots of ways, and there are at least three kinds that you might need. Photographic posters are basically just big prints, and their quality can be excellent; they are best used inside – in a hotel lobby, say. If you need posters to put on telegraph poles and fences, you'd get them *silk-screened* to last longer. If you need posters to *sell* to fans, you'll get them *printed*, so they'll be affordable.

Photographic posters of you or your group can be made from any good photograph, and can be used to promote your band at the site of your job. Check with local printers to get the best prices, and look for special offers that camera shops may run. If you just need one or two posters, you can order them from companies that advertise monthly in photo magazines.

For a good poster, start with a *very good* photograph. Be sure it's as sharp as possible, and is on glossy paper. Don't have a poster made from a very contrasty picture, because it will get even more contrasty; that is, the mid-tones will tend to disappear and the poster will look too harsh.

To present your large photo effectively, have it mounted on foam-core or similar material at a picture-frame shop, and sprayed with a protective coating. Display the poster on an easel or in the window of the club or restaurant where you're working.

Many silk-screen printers do both T-shirts and posters, though some specialise in one or the other, so check the Yellow Pages for a screen printer who does posters. Many offer typesetting capabilities as well, so they can quickly produce a long-lasting, brightly coloured poster for your up-coming blues concert.

If you need a wall-size poster to sell, or give, to fans, check with several printers to get competitive prices. Many quick-copy printers can't print anything larger than A3, so for bigger posters you'll need to find a printer with a web, or sheet-fed, press.

Use the same layout and paste-up techniques we've discussed to prepare camera-ready posters. Use large letters for the headline or caption, and smaller type for the details – and use as few words as possible.

Posters pack punch, so use them.

The Sky's The Limit . . .

Are there more ideas for publicity? Of course. They're invented every day. There's a list of lots of ideas to stimulate your own imagination in Chapter Nineteen.

Here's an example of creative publicity. A few years ago, the Greyhound bus company in Atlanta, USA, ran a very special promotion. For one hour on a certain day, anyone could buy a bus ticket to any destination in the United States for 59 cents. During that hour, Greyhound sold *five thousand* tickets.

Did they lose money? Yes, of course. Fifty-nine cents wouldn't buy a bus ride across Atlanta, much less across the USA.

But look what they gained by this bold publicity ploy:

● Big newspaper articles, with pictures, both before and after the promotion.
● Extensive television coverage, both locally and nationally.
● Extensive radio coverage – including live broadcasts from the bus station and interviews with passengers and company officials on several stations.
● Magazine stories in both consumer and trade publications.

What did Greyhound get by giving away its product? Thousands and thousands of dollars worth of free publicity. The amount lost on cheap tickets is tiny when compared to the extensive, positive national publicity they got.

They also got people talking about bus travel. During the same week, US airlines were offering $59 fares, but Greyhound stole the spotlight by massively undercutting them.

Is a 59 cent fare silly? Of course. Did the publicity programme work? Absolutely. What would have happened if the bus company hadn't come up with this publicity idea? Nothing would have happened. There would have been no stories, no talk, no live interviews. All the transport news that week would have gone to the airlines, as usual. But Greyhound took the publicity initiative – and won.

Of course, you're not running a bus company. But you can use the same creative approach. Think big. Be bold. Take risks. Be willing to lose money – in the short run. Don't even be afraid to look silly. Greyhound didn't, and they stole the headlines for days.

CHAPTER EIGHTEEN

BASIC ADVERTISING

Most of the ideas we've discussed so far focus on free publicity. Getting noticed in newspaper articles and encouraging people to talk about your music, for example, are ways to spread the word without spending money.

Why is publicity so helpful for performers? It's simple. You can blow your own horn without breaking the bank. Your message – "look what we're doing" – gets through without your ever buying an ad. And most of your publicity is more believable *because* it's not bought.

Sometimes, though, you'll be able to benefit from advertising – also known as 'paid publicity.' You won't buy full-page ads, nor will you invest in expensive TV time, but you may augment your publicity programme with a bit of well-selected advertising.

Large companies use professional advertising agencies to produce their ads, but your budget won't be enough to interest most agencies. That's no problem, though, since you've already learned how to create your own publicity. The same techniques apply to ads.

Your Audience In pursuing your publicity campaign, you focus on an exact target audience, a precise group that needs to know about your music. You don't want to reach for everyone in town; just aim at those who can make a difference in your career. Thus, your publicity goes to people who can hire you, buy your records, or come to your performances. You'll approach advertising the same way.

There are so many expensive advertising media that you could easily spend all your publicity budget on ads and never reach the right people. You could waste lots and lots of money on high-priced advertising that looks good – but doesn't work. It's done every day.

Before you even think about buying advertising, ask again, "Who needs to know about my music? How can I reach them at the lowest cost?"

Do you want to reach corporate meeting planners? Nightclub owners? Booking agents? If so, you wouldn't use newspaper ads or radio commercials, because those mass media aren't targeted at your prospects. Of course booking agents read the newspaper and listen to the radio, but so do hundreds of thousands of people who don't need to get your message. Why pay to reach all those extras?

What Should an Ad Do?

Different kinds of advertising have different aims. *Image-building ads* promote a brand name in general terms, with no specific event in mind. Full page car ads in slick magazines are a good example – they promote a brand, but not a dealer or a sale price. Since your publicity is already doing this for you – raising your profile – at little cost, you probably won't need image-building ads.

Specific event advertising tells about something concrete – a concert, a new record or a grand opening. Small newspaper ads to promote club appearances and concerts are examples of this kind of advertising, and the money you spend producing flyers, hand-outs and posters could be considered 'advertising expenditure,'even though these items are part of your low-cost publicity campaign. The line between publicity and advertising is not always a sharp one.

Continuing ads such as Yellow Pages listings or directory entries help people locate you. Maybe a prospective client knows your name – but not your telephone number. A Yellow Pages ad could send him directly to you.

What kind of advertising do *you* need? Maybe none. Or maybe quite a bit. We'll discuss a few possibilities that might help. Choose carefully, though, and think about how you're spending your money.

It's important to remember that advertising sales-people work on commission – if they sell ads, they make money. Don't expect them to give objective information about whether or not you need an ad. They'll always say yes, and they'll have reams of facts and figures to show how their ads will help you.

A good ad is really more of an *investment* than an expenditure. It should pay for itself, and more. So, a good ad doesn't really cost anything in the long run. The difficulty lies in deciding which ads will be good, and which ones won't work. How do you know what to do? Simple research will help you decide.

Another Course in the Media University

You're already keeping a cuttings file of good publicity ideas for study. When your local newspaper runs an interesting profile of a local actor, you should automatically ask, "How did he get that article written? How can I do the same?"

Now take the same approach with advertising. Use the same free 'media university' to learn what is likely to work for you. The reason is: *in the world of small-time advertising, there are no secrets.*

What does that mean? Simply that advertisers who have limited budgets *must* spend wisely; they can only afford advertising that works. (Large advertisers, by contrast, often have enough money to do the kind of *image advertising* that's not designed to yield specific results.)

Doing the following Publicity Practice will help you decide if ads are effective for other people in the entertainment business. If something works for them, it should work for you.

Publicity practice

Start a cuttings file for *competitors' ads*. Look in special sections of the newspaper (entertainment guides, and so on), and read speciality newspapers and advertising circulars. Look for ads from other musicians, performers, and arts or drama groups. Pay special attention to those whose target audience matches yours.

Cut out the ads and *record the date of each one*. If you see the same, or a similar ad, repeated every week or month, you can be pretty sure it's working – but you can't draw any conclusions from just one ad. What you're looking for in your competitors' ads is *continuity*.

Perhaps you see a slick, well-designed ad in a local business paper for a jazz trio –

trying to sell its music for business meetings. You know that the ad cost several hundred pounds to produce and run. Was it worth it to the trio?

How can you find out if this ad generated enough jobs to pay for itself? Look at the next several issues of the magazine. If the trio repeats the ad for several months, it's almost certainly working. (However, if the leader of this trio is independently wealthy, such research is invalid. Be alert for such extraneous facts.)

Research Before You Leap

Looking for repeated ads is a useful, simple way to judge an ad's effectiveness, but there are other routes you can use to decide if an advertisement would be worthwhile.

Ask the person who's running an ad if it's working. Perhaps a competitor will tell you, perhaps not. Perhaps he'll tell you an ad is working even if it's not, or vice versa, just to throw you off the track. You'll have to use common sense and intuition to decide if you're getting good information.

As you know, many musicians are jealous of their success and nervous about losing their clients and jobs. If you ask for information, make it very clear that you are not a threat, that your target is a different market entirely. Explain that your efforts won't infringe on their turf.

Thus, try to find another musician who advertises, but whose music isn't enough like yours to be directly competitive. "Hello, George. This is Mary Smith. I have a pop/rock band, and I know that you're in a country band. I've seen your ads in the local press, and I wondered how they're working out for you." If Mary makes it clear that she's not trying to steal the country-music market from George, he may be happy to tell her about his advertising results. Or, he may not.

You can also talk to the advertising department of the media you're interested in. Remember that above all they want to sell you an ad, so don't believe everything they tell you, but ask anyway. Request a demographic breakdown of their readers – age, sex, education, income and so on – to see if it matches your target audience.

And you can even ask ad sales-people about the success of your competitors' advertising. Perhaps they'll tell you, if they know, how the ads for George's country band are working. It doesn't hurt to ask.

If you do decide to buy an ad, don't sign a long-term contract until you've proved, from experience, that the ad will work for you. Even though the rates are much lower for ads that repeat regularly, don't obligate yourself until you've tested a few ads and carefully monitored the results.

If you're thinking about running ads in newspapers, magazines or on the radio, call the advertising department of each media outlet you're considering and ask for rate information.

Rates vary with circulation, type of paper, size of ad, how often the ad runs (one insertion costs the most, of course), whether the ad runs week-days or Sunday, and other factors. As a hypothetical example, a local weekly with a circulation of 40,000 might charge £125 for an eighth of a page (four by three inches, which is technically 12 column inches), while a provincial daily with a circulation of 27,500 might charge £100 for the same size ad, and a large metropolitan daily, with combined morning and evening circulation of 439,000 might charge £625. To get a true comparative cost in such a case, divide the cost by the circulation to get the cost per thousand (or *cpm*). Remember, large circulation may not be the most relevant consideration for your specialised message, and the lowest *cpm* may not be the best deal; analyse the readership carefully to be sure it matches your needs.

Test, Test, Test

All smart advertisers are *testing experts*. They tabulate results to learn which ads work, and what can be done to improve them – and which ones aren't effective at all.

You must do the same thing. In fact, you're already testing each time you ask a prospect, "Where did you hear about my band?" *You must know which publicity or advertising methods are working, and which ones aren't.* If you don't keep test results, your publicity and advertising could be wasting your time, effort and money.

Let's say that you've bought a classified ad in the Sunday newspaper. The ad costs £25 a week, and you've signed up for four weeks. (Too short a run won't give accurate results, so you've committed £100 to this test, deciding that a month will give a fair trial.)

From now on, for the next couple of months, you must be sure to ask each prospective client, "Where did you learn about our music?" – and to record the response. Pay particular attention, during your test, to those who cite the Sunday paper as their source. Record the results for each ad on a separate sheet, and be sure to keep careful records.

Perhaps the ad generates 10 calls a week, but no one books your band. The ad seems to be arousing interest, but maybe your music doesn't match the callers' expectations. Or maybe your follow-up material is faulty. You might reword the ad, or change your selling pitch, because you should certainly book a job or two from 10 enquiries.

Perhaps you don't get any enquiries at all that can be traced to the newspaper ad. For some reason, the ad isn't working. Drop it, and concentrate your efforts somewhere else.

Maybe you get 10 calls because of the ad – and book five jobs. In this case, the ad pays for itself many times over, and you should continue to run it until it stops working. You might, from time to time, change the wording slightly to experiment with different emphasis, but don't change it every week. Continuity is important, and the same weekly ad helps build your name recognition.

Judging how much to spend on advertising – if anything at all – requires close attention to the results of each ad. And you can't stop testing, so get in the habit of tracking the effectiveness of each ad – and publicity ploy – you try.

A famous saying in advertising is, "I'm sure I waste half the money I spend on ads – but the trouble is that I don't know which half." Testing helps you know what works.

The two principal kinds of ads you could use are specific ones that promote a particular event, and long-term ads that work for months or years. We'll discuss both. *Specific* events can be advertised through small ads in newspapers or with flyers, posters, hand-bills and banners. *Long-lasting media* include the Yellow Pages, other directories, and advertising speciality items that you give away.

Newspaper Ads: Think Small

Newspapers sell advertising by the inch, or by fractions of pages. They also have *classified* sections that charge for each word. You'll rarely, if ever, buy a large ad; the cost is usually hundreds of pounds, at least. But you may, in some instances, use small ones. Here are some ideas.

Study the small ads you're cutting out for the Publicity Practice earlier in this chapter. Many papers and magazines have lots of one- and two-inch ads, some of which are very effective. Study the ones you've saved that reappear. They're working, even if they're small. (Such ads are called *display* advertising, as opposed to classified ads.)

Small ads usually don't try to tell the whole story. They just try to attract attention and a phone call from prospective clients. Small ads rely on one- or two-word headlines to grab attention, so you can't afford to waste a word. A one-inch ad captioned "FIREWOOD" delivers a direct message, and if you need firewood, you'll notice it. You can learn useful techniques from any effective ad, so when you're studying the ones that reappear, don't limit yourself to entertainment. Many small business-people and professionals face the same budget limitations you do, and spend advertising money carefully. Watch what they do.

Would a one-inch ad captioned MUSIC be effective? Probably not, because music is such a general term. Something more specific, however, like DIXIELAND, or SALSA or JAM SESSION, would attract the attention of people who enjoy those particular kinds of music.

You can design and produce the ad yourself, or have the newspaper do it for you. If you do it yourself, get their house-style sheet, and be sure you understand the specifications; measurements may be in *picas* rather than inches, and there will be other technical terms that could be confusing.

It's easier, especially at first, to let the paper design and typeset your ad, though you should provide a sketch of your idea as a guide. Make the sketch as close to the finished size and proportion as you can, and look at a proof before the ad is printed. Most papers charge very little if anything to prepare such small ads.

It's Classified

If your paper has special classified sections devoted to nightlife, wedding services, business needs, and so on, you may find them to be useful. Since classifieds are divided into precise headings, people who read them are already interested in each category. Nobody reads the classifieds for fun.

Like small display ads, classifieds don't try to tell the whole story – all they need to do is attract interest and curiosity. You tell your story when you answer the phone – a classified ad is only intended to make your phone ring with prospective clients.

How should you use classifieds? Suppose you're a piano teacher, and after an initial test period, you've satisfied yourself that your classified ad in the local weekly is bringing you new pupils. Now you should decide to run the ad continuously. Classifieds are inexpensive, and they're *always there*. Thus, a reader who isn't interested in taking piano lessons in June can change his mind in October – and still find your ad. When the price per ad is low, continuity is important.

Even if you run the classified every week, there will probably be weeks when you don't get a single new call, so in that sense you'll probably 'waste' some of your advertising budget. But you won't know in advance which week will be good and which won't get any response, so overall it's better to run the ad constantly. And one new student can pay for a year's ads.

Remember OPM

OPM is an abbreviation for *Other People's Money.* When you're planning newspaper advertising, use *OPM* when you can.

If your band is working in a nightclub that advertises each week in the Saturday newspaper, encourage the club owner to mention your name. Tell him about your loyal following, your fans who want to know where you're playing. Let him promote his club – and your band – at the same time.

If you're a piano teacher, try to do the same thing with a music shop, or even a piano manufacturer. Perhaps you're presenting an in-store demonstration, or giving a concert on a particular make of piano. Contact the sponsoring shop or manufacturer, and ask their ad manager to advertise your performance, tying it in with his product. You'll both benefit, and it won't cost you anything.

Newspaper ads can be useful if you're very careful with where and how you spend your money. Don't forget, though, what happens to yesterday's paper, so be sure that the ad you buy is really the ad you need.

Will Their Fingers do the Walking

Mrs. Johnson, whose daughter is getting married, has never hired a band before. In fact, she's never spoken face-to-face with a live musician. Now, however, she needs to find a band for the wedding reception but she doesn't know how to go about it. She's never met a booking agent, and she certainly doesn't know you.

She thinks, "Aha. The Yellow Pages." She looks under 'Musicians.' Does she find your name? Should she?

For many businesses, Yellow Pages listings are very important. In fact, many businesses and professionals do no other advertising except for their phone directory entries.

A simple line-listing in Yellow Pages is free to business phone subscribers, but can cost up to about £70 for an ordinary domestic subscriber. An *ad* can cost anything from £70 to £5,000, depending on the size.

Despite the expense, should you be listed? After all, if an ad pays for itself, it's worth it. Again, you'll be guided by research. Check the Yellow Pages under 'Musicians,' 'Entertainers,' and other listings that may be relevant – 'Wedding Services,' for example, if weddings are your speciality. See if other musicians are listed.

If you find such entries, simply call them and ask if the Yellow Pages ads work, or see if the ads are repeated year after year.

If you have an established name that's widely known in your area – Joe's Band, The Blues Kings, or whatever, it may pay you to be listed so prospective clients who already know your name can locate you.

The standard advertising theory the Yellow Pages uses is that every listed business stands an equal chance – shoppers don't know you and can't tell over the phone who is established and who isn't. By this theory, those with the bigger, dominant ads will get more calls.

The Yellow Pages may be very useful to you. Or it may just be money that you can't afford. Do as much research as you can before committing yourself.

Ultimately, you'll have to take a chance with Yellow Pages ads – you really can't know whether an ad will work without trying. To make it more difficult, you'll have to decide well in advance, since telephone directories are annual publications.

If you do get a Yellow Pages listing, try diligently to keep the number active. It is *bad* publicity for callers to find that "this number has been disconnected." They'll assume the worst about you, so if you get listed, stay listed.

Flyers and Hand-bills

Flyers have always been a great advertising medium for performers. They're like little posters, but are so inexpensive that you can cover an area with them. They can be considered to be low-cost publicity, of course, but we'll discuss them in this chapter since they're also like little ads, promoting specific events.

Flyers and hand-bills are really just small posters, usually A4, and you can make them yourself. Use transfer type, have the copy typeset, or even use a black marker to hand-write the finished copy. A quick-copy printer, or even a photocopy machine, will inexpensively produce as many flyers as you want – on bright paper, if appropriate, to attract attention.

Where would you use flyers and hand-bills? Everywhere. Put them on car windscreens, in shop windows, on school, library or launderette noticeboards. Hire teenagers to distribute them door to door. You can even fold them over, staple them together, and mail them.

You can use hand-bills to make special offers, or to do last-minute publicity for a concert. Wherever there are crowds, flyers and hand-bills are effective.

What should a hand-bill or flyer (or poster) tell? As little as possible. Study the professionally produced billboards in your area. Even though they cost thousands of pounds to create, they use only a few words. Advertisers often go for *impact*, not *information*.

You should take the same approach. Limit yourself to the 'who, what, where, when and how much' that your audience needs to know. A short headline, set in the biggest possible type, will grab attention, and the copy (set in smaller type, of course) should give exact, succinct information.

LIKE BIG BAND MUSIC? Join the Capital City Big Band for dancing and fun. Newcastle Civic Centre, Saturday, April 11, 8.00-12.00. Tickets only £3.50 at the door

CARNIVAL. The Fabulous Songbirds play classic Rock'n'Roll. Saturday Afternoon, June 4, Clapham Common. Benefits Cancer Research.

PIANO LESSONS. Experienced teacher with advanced degrees will come to your home. Amy, 123-4567 for information

In each case the headline grabs attention, and the smaller type gives the fewest possible details to complete the story. The big, simple headlines will attract people who are interested in each subject – big bands, carnivals or piano lessons. Don't use flyers (or posters) to tell the *entire* story – just get their attention, and give the main message.

Flyers need to be noticed, and coloured – even fluorescent – paper stock can be attention-getting and effective. You might experiment with unusual, or smaller, sizes, but be aware of the printing, cutting and trimming charges.

Remember the KISS rule and use it in preparing your flyers and hand-bills. "Keep It Simple, Sir" and leave out as much as you can. Just attract attention, tell 'who, what, when, where and how much,' and your flyer will have done its job.

Banners

Banners that stretch across the street or a shop-front attract lots of attention. You can make them yourself using paint, cloth and rope, or you can have sign-painters prepare them for you. Most screen printers will prepare professional-looking long-lasting banners.

A banner must be *timely* to be effective. And if it is hung where the event will take place, so much the better. If you're planning a street party, village fête, or grand opening, use a banner to mark the spot.

You'll have to get permission to stretch a banner across a street; check with the local council. Get permission, then, and use them when you can, because a colourful banner stretched between two trees can be an excellent way of publicising that concert in the park.

Advertising Specialities

Do you have a trade calendar on your wall? Is there a book of matches from a restaurant in your pocket? Are you writing with a pen inscribed with an insurance agent's name? These are *advertising specialities*, and they're a great medium for you to consider.

There are, incredibly, over 15,000 different items in the advertising speciality market. Most of them can be imprinted with your name or message, and many are inexpensive enough to be given away.

This is a different kind of advertising, with a different purpose. You don't use such give-aways to *sell*, but to *remind* people that you're still around or thank them for using your services. These little items don't tell your story; they just carry your name.

To get an idea of what's available, request catalogues from a few of the companies listed in the Yellow Pages under "Promotional items." You'll be surprised at how many firms compete in this area, and you'll be amazed at the number of products you can buy.

You can have your name or logo imprinted on car stickers, shirts, guitar picks, binders, calendars, Christmas cards, pens, pencils, key rings, buttons, matchbooks, lighters, balloons, tote bags, umbrellas, mugs, paperweights, scratch pads, carrier bags, rulers, and thousands of other items.

Is this kind of advertising effective? Yes, if you choose wisely and don't spend too much money. Before you buy, however, ask:

1. *Is it useful?* A wooden penny imprinted with your name might be cute, but what will it do? It will be lost or thrown away within a week. A scratch pad, however, with your logo, name and message printed on it, will be used constantly. A comedian I know gives giant four-inch cubes of scratch pads to all his clients, and each time they write a note they think of him. The recipient of each note also gets the built-in publicity message.

2. *Is it inexpensive?* Don't waste a lot of money on these items if you can't afford it. If you're choosing between felt-tip pens that cost 15p each and coffee mugs that cost nearer a pound, decide how far your budget will go. You could give away 250 pens for the same cost as 50 mugs. Which would your clients use more often?

3. *Is it unusual?* As useful as calendars are, most people don't need more than one or two – and plenty of businesses will provide those. Search for a free gift that's unique as well as useful.

4. *Is the price competitive?* Get several quotes from different suppliers, and don't buy more than you need. Specialities are like printing: the more you buy, the less expensive each unit is. But can you really use 2000 pens with your name on them, even if they only cost 7 pence apiece?

Today's Car Sticker Is . . .

Car stickers are a very popular speciality item – almost like T-shirts for cars – and they're an effective advertising medium. You use them on your own car (and instrument case), of course, and give them to fans, supporters and anyone else who's interested.

Silk-screening is the best way to produce high-quality stickers, but you'll have the same set-up charges as for T-shirts. Screened stickers last the longest, and can handle very fine detail. (Again, find these printers in the Yellow Pages under "Screen process printers.")

Offset printing produces stickers that don't last as well, but they're cheaper to buy. Most printed stickers will fade after about 90 days in the sun – and your long-term message may disappear with it.

Do-it-yourself stickers can be made with a simple kit consisting of a metal backing plate, a blank piece of vinyl, and magnetic letters that stick in place. Once you've spelled out your message with the magnetised letters, you use a special spray paint to colour the sticker, let it dry, and remove the letters. Such stickers are very inexpensive to produce, but are time-consuming, and don't look very exciting because the colours are usually harsh and they all use the same type style.

Car stickers are so popular for serious – and funny – messages, that you can get lots of mileage from them. If you can think of a clever message, or a pun, that's short and simple – and publicises your music – why not use it? You're going to be driving around anyway, so your car might as well become an advertising vehicle. With car stickers, your advertising expenditure will go a long way.

To Repeat

You're blowing your own horn in as many ways as possible, and you may find that inexpensive advertising will be an important component in your overall plan. Always remember, though, that advertising should *pay for itself*; if it doesn't, it's not helping you. No matter how good-looking or slick an ad is, it's worthless if it doesn't sell.

Actually, of course, a poor ad is worse than worthless because it brings no benefits, and costs money to produce and run.

If an ad works, use it. If it doesn't, concentrate your efforts on other ways of getting noticed. When you use advertising wisely, it can help, but it should never be more than a part of your entire publicity programme.

CHAPTER NINETEEN

EVENTS TO PUBLICISE

By now you have the tools and knowledge you need to publicise your music –
in the media, by word of mouth, with T-shirts, and in lots of other ways.

Throughout this book we've used *brainstorming* as a way to discover ideas
and get out of mental ruts. It's a great technique to find, or create, events to
publicise; brainstorming often provides the creative kick you need. It gives you
an idea, and you suddenly realise, "Aha! That's it!"

You know you'll benefit from publicity – that's the point of this book. But
you also know you need a hook, a peg, a point of interest where your music
intersects with a bigger idea or a popular issue. It's up to you to find connections
that work.

Here are more ideas. Some will quickly bring good publicity, others may not
work at all. Don't be discouraged, however, if each project you undertake
doesn't result in all the publicity you want, every time. Just keep trying.

Remember, every organisation, business, committee, school, individual
entrepreneur, and government group is after publicity, too. They're spending just
as much time and effort as you are – to tell the world about *their* causes and
projects. You can't expect to win every time.

Keep looking for new angles, fresh ideas, unique approaches, outrageous
stunts. Watch what publicity professionals do to attract attention. Perhaps you
won't hire sky-writing planes, or parachute onto Centre Court during
Wimbledon, or even burn guitars on stage. But you can profit from planned
events. Planned, that is, with publicity in mind.

This chapter presents ideas for music-related publicity. Use them as a
springboard to jolt your own brainstorming, and apply them when they fit your
own needs. Some of these ideas have been discussed earlier; they are included
again to provide a quick review of the myriad ways you can get noticed. The
exciting thing is that there's no limit to your creativity, so this list is really just a
beginning, a nudge to get you started.

Are you a classical musician? A rock band? A country group? A cabaret singer?
Do you write songs? Teach improvisation – or classical guitar? Many of these
ideas apply to all different kinds of music; others will be limited to one genre or
another.

Can you invent something to celebrate with music? Of course. Whether you're
working in a club or directing a marching band, you can come up with good
ideas. Maybe it hasn't been done before. Then you'll have a 'World Première' to
publicise. Or maybe it's been done each year – but without your music. Then
you can join the tradition.

You know what catches an editor's eye: it's a hook, an angle that interests him
– and his audiences. You're creative, so go ahead and devise your own events to

publicise if you can. That's exactly what public relations professionals get paid to do.

So use this chapter as a nudge to your brainstorming, or a quick review of the ideas and techniques discussed in this book, or an overview of what publicity is all about. It's up to you.

Is It News?

You're already working on events to publicise with a press release and with other techniques that you now know. Some of these events need the full treatment; others require subtlety. Be sure to include anything that's:

An anniversary. Is your band celebrating its 15th year of playing rock and roll together? How many times have you played 'Louie, Louie'? How many clubs have you worked? It's a story. Other anniversaries to note include

- The date of a famous composition
- The birth, or death, of a well-known composer, artist or performer
- The fifth birthday of the bistro where you play guitar
- The fifth year you've played for a company dinner-dance
- The 75th birthday of a church, theatre concert hall, pipe organ or whatever; birthdays are anniversaries to celebrate

A social event. Has your band been booked to play a May Ball in Oxford? Publicise it in your town, and in Oxford. Social events include

- Annual country-club functions
- Débutante balls and parties
- Large weddings and receptions
- Annual parties and fêtes sponsored by prominent people and organisations
- Openings of galleries, elegant restaurants, country clubs
- Black-tie events related to concerts, showings, fashion shows, fund-raisers for charities

Be sensitive to what's appropriate when publicising your part in someone else's event – don't make too big a deal of the fact that you're playing for a deb party, say, but do let the society columnist of your paper know that you're an important, continuing part of the social whirl. You don't want to offend a client by publicising *her* party for your purposes, but you should subtly spread the word.

A civic project. Are you donating your music to raise money for a park? The homeless? A community centre? Other civic projects include

- Participation in a neighbourhood clean-up day
- Working as an unpaid music therapist for a community mental health centre
- Teaching free, or at reduced price, poor (or handicapped) people
- Joining city leaders to celebrate an important local anniversary

A special achievement. Have you been made principal flute in your orchestra? Has your album gone Platinum? Did you succeed in an audition for Kent Opera?

Also note such achievements as

- Winning any kind of contest
- Receiving any kind of scholarship
- Performing in a prestigious venue – your first Wigmore Hall recital
- Getting a job through competitive evaluation – passing the first round of a national audition
- Having a song or book published
- Signing a record contract

A forthcoming event. Is your annual Christmas concert scheduled for December 10th? Are your piano pupils giving a recital? Is your band playing for the opening of a new club in town? Also, of course, publicise such events as

- Your first night at a new club
- Your band is the opening act for a major rock concert
- The first performance in a new or renovated auditorium, club, concert hall
- The première performance by your new or re-formed band

A celebrity or out-of-town group is involved. Is the local Music Club sponsoring a workshop by Carl Davis? A concert by Van Cliburn? A festival featuring the Delmé String Quartet? A fund-raiser with the Count Basie Band? Other celebrity-related events are

- Guest appearances by famous musicians with any band, at any venue
- Speeches, presentations, awards, given to – or by – the celebrity
- Guest appearances featuring famous former members of your band
- Record- or book-signing events sponsored by your organisation, usually in conjunction with a record company or publisher

An introduction. Is your record finally coming out? Are you introducing new band uniforms – that were paid for by the members themselves? Did you build your own five-string bass from a solid block of oak – and you're introducing it with a special concert? Introductory events can include

- Presentation of a new band member, soloist, conductor or arranger
- The grand opening of your teaching studio, renovated concert hall, redecorated music shop, or expanded band-room
- The first performance – or first *local* one, anyway – of a new, or famous, or newly discovered work

A personnel change. Is a new conductor making his début? Is the leader of the orchestra retiring? Have you hired a recent Pan's Conservatoire graduate to teach at your studio? Also publicise these:

- A new player of exceptional ability joining your group
- A new management agreement or agency contract
- A new band director, assistant director, music teacher – any addition to your group or staff

**Can it be
Featured**

As you know, there's often little distinction between *news* and *feature* material – and feature stories are frequently longer, with more pictures. *Lifestyle* pieces are popular with the press, so your ideas can generate good publicity if they're:

Unique. Is yours the first all-girl rock band in town? Are you reverting to unamplified, acoustic jazz? Have you built a pipe organ from parts bought at the ironmongers? Do you play the glass harmonica?

Trendy. Aerobics, walking, jogging, macrobiotics, digital electronics, video art, holograms – these are trends that catch the media's attention. Does your band do aerobic exercises together? Have you commissioned a hologram to display on stage? Have you composed and produced a tape of jogging music – to be used 'on the road' with personal Walkman-type players?

First or earliest. Is your band the first in town to do away with 'real' drummers? Are you playing a violin that was made in 1837? Does your 'Early Music Consort' use hand-made instruments to re-create the hits of the 15th century?

Inspiring. Did you overcome arthritis to learn the piano? Did you take up the flute because your doctor wanted you to exercise your lungs? Did you start writing songs to ease your post-divorce depression? Did you succeed?

Largest. Forget the musical quality – is your college music department sponsoring a Play-a-Thon at which 200 local students will simultaneously play 'Für Elise'? Does your brass band have 150 members?

Ethnic. If you have knowledge of ethnic cultures use it. What is a Greek restaurant without Greek music? Do you play Japanese, Chinese, Indonesian, Russian, Italian, or any other special kind of music? Tie it in with restaurants, churches, festivals. Combine it with costumes, foods, drama, other arts.

Do You Have a Date?
We've talked about this one before, but it offers such creative possibilities that it deserves another mention. Virtually every day of the year can be celebrated. Sometimes the anniversary is serious, sometimes it's frivolous. It doesn't matter; if you can link up with a birthday or anniversary, you share the publicity.

Do It
Plan an event, put on a party, make a statement with your actions. Perhaps you can do the entire project, or maybe you need to find a co-sponsor. You can publicise an event that's:

Extraordinary. Try for a *Guinness Book of Records* entry with the world's loudest trumpet solo, biggest dance contest, longest version of 'Shout' or largest Christmas carol sing-along.

Enriching. Demonstrate your kind of music at a community centre, prison, old people's home, inner-city school, or youth club.

Free. Why not hold a chamber music concert in the park – or from the deck of a sailing boat moored in the harbour? Could you give weekly midday jazz, folk or classical concerts in a city-centre office building? Could your choir, band or group perform at a shopping mall for Christmas or other festivals.

Worthwhile. Did you give free saxophone lessons to deprived kids? Make a local record to raise money for displaced workers? Hold monthly musical evenings at a nursing home?

Festive. Hold your own 'Old-Time Blues Festival,' or 'Old-Time Barbershop Quartet Festival.' Any kind of music that can attract several groups can have a festival – especially if it can be called 'Old-Time...' Perhaps it could be competitive, with celebrity judges to award prizes. A battle of the bands, a jazz-trio play-off, a country fiddling contest – all will attract musicians, crowds and publicity. Maybe it shouldn't be competitive, but an evening of a particular kind of music, just for fun.

You could hold such a festival at a large park (perhaps co-sponsored by the local council), at a community college or cultural centre, or even in a hotel ballroom (if you can find a sponsor to underwrite the expenses).

More Miscellaneous Ideas

These, and hundreds of similar ideas, can be turned into good publicity – and can also be enjoyable activities for you and your group. Include a hook to assure media attention, of course, but be sure that the event itself is interesting, fulfilling and fun.

And when you've planned an event – with that interesting hook – don't forget to publicise it to all the usual sources. Let them know what you're doing, so they can tell the world.

Sponsor a dance contest. The Twist, Jerk, Shag, Waltz, Jitterbug, Charleston or anything else can draw attention, and crowds. Square dances and clogging exhibitions can be popular, too. As discussed in Chapter Sixteen, you can enhance the publicity value of such an event by using local celebrities to judge – TV people, sports figures, politicians, or prominent business-people. Or, of course, you could ask dance (or even ballet) instructors to judge, which could be an interesting juxtaposition of formal training and spontaneous energy.

Hold open rehearsals. Your band, chorus or orchestra can invite music lovers to a free rehearsal, serve coffee, and even present an explanatory programme. You could also schedule regular jam sessions. Many non-professionals and former musicians like to play and sing, and would love the chance to perform with you. This idea can work as well for single pianists as for amateur orchestras; welcome the amateurs to an 'open microphone' and watch your popularity soar.

Or try a classical sing-along. This is often done with the *Messiah* at Christmas, but you could do the same thing with Gilbert and Sullivan, and other popular works. People love to sing, so give them a chance. If you're part of an amateur orchestra, church choir, or school music department, this would be a relatively simple project for you, since you already have access to performance halls – and it would directly involve lots of people in your music.

Pick a charitable cause that hasn't yet become popular, and donate your music for a fund-raiser, dance, banquet or picnic. The zoo, botanical gardens, a hospital, children's home, old people's home, inner-city community, restoration project, a disease-research organisation, or many other good projects will benefit from your gift. (You'll benefit, too, by sharing your talent.)

Theme parties are always great, whether you sponsor them yourselves or work with another organisation. The possibilities are unlimited – Costume parties, Murder Mystery – whatever you can devise will work. The more effort you put into such events – with costumes, special food, decorations, as well as music – the more publicity you'll generate.

Hold reunion events. Invite all former members of your group to reassemble for jam sessions or concerts. This idea will work well for any long-established group – school bands, church choirs, amateur orchestras, dance bands and even barbershop quartets.

Search, with appropriate publicity of course, for the *oldest or most famous* graduate of your group. Is an MP a former member of your dance band? Did an 82-year-old clarinet player come to this year's reunion – and take a sizzling solo?

Hold a musical garage sale. Have everyone in your group bring old music, records, instruments, accessories, magazines, books and so on. You'll be surprised at the depth of local interest in music – and in garage sales.

Sponsor a music auction if you can get enough donated material. You'll benefit particularly from items used by celebrities – guitar picks from Mick Jagger, Bruce Springsteen's T-shirt, James Galway's coffee cup. Anything musical can be auctioned – but items with local or national celebrity associations will bring the most money. (Acquiring such items, however, takes lots of advance planning. Booking agents and record companies can help you find addresses for celebrities' management. Write to them, explain what you're doing, emphasise that it's for a *very worthwhile cause* and that the celebrity will receive good, nearly free publicity. Ask for a donation of something that can be auctioned off – anything from a coffee cup, T-shirt, or autographed albums on up will be saleable.)

Hold a musical art exhibition. Collect serious – and whimsical – art that's music-related and show it in a mall, bank lobby or shop window. Make a sculpture from all your broken drumsticks. Show off your collection of antique instruments. Have the school art students draw their impressions of a concert. Display your photos of famous jazz, rock or country musicians.

Issue an annual report for your group. This works especially well for larger organisations like recording studios. Make it a newsletter format, with photos included of your major activities during the year.

Write an article for the local paper. Make it a list-type piece – they're easy to write (for instance, 'Ten Ways to Help a Piano Survive Your Children'; 'The 15 Funniest Events in My Musical Life'). Or write how-to articles for music trade magazines. 'How to Hold a Celebrity Music Auction,' or 'How to Record a Demo

Tape.' All magazines like 'how-to' pieces. Other ideas: 'How to Form Your First Rock Band,' 'How to Improvise – for Classical Pianists,' 'How to Move Equipment Without Hurting Your Back,' 'How to Understand Today's Music.'

If you are a part-time musician, work for publicity in your 'real' career's professional journals. If you're a banker, try for a profile in banking magazines about your fifties rock band. If your entire band is made up of stockbrokers, the interest you could get from the business pages will pay big publicity dividends – a valuable commodity for any musician.

If your profession offers this sort of chance to develop publicity, use it.

Look for interesting personal hooks from every member of your band. Was your drummer's father also a drummer? Does your mother sing in the local opera company – and hate the rock music you play? (Or does she love it?) Can you trace your musical heritage back through four generations?

Produce a historical festival complete with period music, food, costumes, drama and sports. This kind of project needs co-sponsors, but can be very successful.

Perhaps the club or restaurant where you work could co-sponsor such an event on a small scale – a '1935 night,' for example, with music, costumes and prices from that year. Add a look-alike contest – for movie stars and singers from that era. Perhaps senior citizens, who remember those years, could judge such a contest – and generate more publicity.

If it's the 75th anniversary of a local club, find out what music was popular that year, and offer to take part in any official celebration.

Prepare a programme to celebrate a local composer or artist. Write a show, prepare a programme, produce a concert to honour a local musical hero. Work with the local Tourist Board – they're interested in local promotions, too.

Get involved in political events that affect music, or the arts in general. Organise a petition, for instance, to protest at the withdrawal of state support from the local symphony orchestra.

Hold a 'demonstration' – with picket signs, or sandwich boards. Publicise your concert, or the weekly jam session, or raise local awareness of your music by holding a 'positive protest.' Check with the police to see if permission is required, or you may really make news by being arrested – and you probably don't want publicity *that* badly.

Be a pavement musician for a day. (Get permission first if it's needed.) Play on a busy street corner, at an underground station, on the front steps of the town hall to publicise an event. You'll get noticed – just don't get arrested.

Do a one-off promotion for a widely supported music project – an orchestral concert, say, or summer concerts in the park – by playing on *buses, trains or ferries*. Wake up the morning commuters by strolling through the bus playing your guitar – or have the soloist from your choir sing a couple of duets to people waiting for a commuter train. Outlandish? Of course. Effective? Certainly.

You get the idea, don't you? Be creative, unique, first, last, newest, oldest, youngest – whatever. Just do something interesting, follow the steps to make your activity known, and you'll get noticed.

Will you be embarrassed to blow your own horn?

Why should you be? You're proud of your music, aren't you? You enjoy performing, don't you? And people are entertained, uplifted or excited by your music, aren't they? If you'd rather sit at home alone and play sad songs for yourself, go ahead. But if you want people to notice you, hire you, *pay you*, you've got to let them know that you exist.

Because in the long run, if you don't tell them – who will?

PRESS RELEASE

Starting today, thousands of musicians are taking a new approach to their careers. They're finding new opportunities and markets for their music — by blowing their own horns. They're working to get themselves noticed by more clients and larger audiences.

"We've practised scales and songs for years," says Joe, of the famous Joe's Band. "Now we're going to practise public relations, too. We already play great music, and now we're going to tell the world about it."

Musicians like Joe are using the information from *Getting Noticed* to link their music to interesting issues and ideas. They're learning that sitting alone in their rooms won't build a career, so they're taking their messages to the public.

These energetic musicians are producing press releases and writing feature stories to spread the word. They're making car stickers and T-shirts to promote their music. They're designing handsome letterheads and unique business cards that demonstrate their professionalism, and they're creating posters and flyers, hosting parties, making sales calls, and using dozens of other techniques to let people know about their music.

No longer are musicians sitting around waiting for the phone to ring. They're generating interest in their music — and bookings — by telling the world what they do.

Performers of all sorts, from folk fiddlers to orchestral violinists, now realise that nothing happens until they play for an audience — and that finding that audience is, ultimately, up to them.

"I know I'm creative," says Joe (of Joe's Band). "I just never thought before about the importance of being creative in areas other than music. Now you're going to hear about us everywhere you look: newspapers, magazines, TV — even telegraph poles. Joe's Band is getting noticed. And we're doing it ourselves."

INDEX

If you have enjoyed this book you will also be interested in the following Omnibus Press titles.

THE CRAFT OF LYRIC WRITING
Sheila Davis
ISBN: 0.7119.1718.3
Order No: OP 45152

MAKING MONEY MAKING MUSIC
James Dearing
ISBN: 0.7119.1721.3
Order No: OP 45186

THE SONGWRITER'S AND MUSICIAN'S GUIDE TO MAKING GREAT DEMOS
Harvey Rachlin
ISBN: 0.7119.1715.9
Order No: OP 45129

MAKING IT IN THE NEW MUSIC BUSINESS
James Riordan
ISBN: 0.7119.1717.5
Order No: OP 45145

WRITING TOGETHER: THE SONGWRITER'S GUIDE TO COLLABORATION
Walter Carter
ISBN: 0.7119.1713.2
Order No: OP 45103

SUCCESSFUL LYRIC WRITING: A STEP-BY-STEP COURSE & WORKBOOK
Sheila Davis
ISBN: 0.7119.1720.5
Order No: OP 45178

PROFIT FROM YOUR MUSIC
James Gibson
ISBN: 0.7119.1716.7
Order No: OP 45137

HOW TO PITCH & PROMOTE YOUR SONGS
Fred Koller
ISBN: 0.7119.1714.0
Order No: OP 45111

THE CRAFT & BUSINESS OF SONGWRITING
John Braheny
ISBN: 0.7119.1820.1
Order No: OP 45418

BREAKS FOR YOUNG BANDS
Ed Berman
ISBN: 0.7119.0978.4
Order No: OP 43926

HOW TO MAKE AND SELL YOUR OWN RECORD
Diane Sward Rapaport
ISBN: 0.7119.0759.5
Order No: AM 39785

HOW TO SUCCEED IN THE MUSIC BUSINESS
Allan Dann & John Underwood
ISBN: 0.86001.454.1
Order No: AM 19977

THE PLATINUM RAINBOW: HOW TO MAKE IT BIG IN THE MUSIC BUSINESS
Bob Monaco & James Riordan
ISBN: 0.7119.1040.5
Order No: OP 44130

Omnibus Press

No. 1 for Rock & Pop Books